TA for Busy People

ALSO BY NELSON BOSWELL

Successful Living Day by Day

TA for Busy People:

How to Use Transactional Analysis at Home and at Work

Nelson Boswell, Ed.D.

FOREWARD BY
STEPHEN KARPMAN M. D.

HARPER & ROW, PUBLISHERS
New York, Hagerstown, San Francisco, London

Greatful acknowledgment is made for permission to reprint material from the following:

"A Prayer for My Daughter," from *Collected Poems* by William Butler Yeats. Copyright 1924 by Macmillan Publishing Co., Inc. Renewed 1952 by Bertha Georgie Yeats. Reprinted with permission of Macmillan Publishing Co., Inc.

The Screwtape Letters by C. S. Lewis. Copyright C. S. Lewis 1942. Reprinted with permission of Macmillan Publishing Co., Inc.

The Abolition of Man. Copyright 1944, 1947 by Macmillan Publishing Co., Inc. Renewed 1972, 1975 by Alfred Cecil Harwood and Arthur Owen Barfield. Reprinted with permission of Macmillan Publishing Co., Inc.

The Prophet by Kahlil Gibran, and *The Doctor and the Soul: From Psychotherapy to Logotherapy,* Second Edition, by Viktor E. Frankl. Translated by Richard and Clara Winston, and reprinted with permission of Alfred A. Knopf, Inc.

Philosopher's Quest by Irwin Edman. Copyright 1947 by Irwin Edman, © renewed 1975 by Meta Markel. Reprinted with permission of The Viking Press.

Orthodoxy by G. K. Chesterton. Reprinted with permission of Dodd, Mead & Company.

The Achieving Society by David McClelland. Published by D. Van Nostrand. Reprinted with permission of the author.

Anxiety and the Executive by Alan N. Schoonmaker. Published by AMACON, a division of American Management Association, Inc. Reprinted with permission of the publisher.

Marital Brinkmanship by Dr. A. H. Chapman. Reprinted with permission of G. P. Putnam & Sons.

Sickness unto Death by Soren Kierkegaard. Reprinted with permission of Princeton University Press.

Surprised by Joy by C. S. Lewis. Reprinted with permission of Harcourt Brace Jovanovich, Inc.

Los Angeles *Times* article by Tom Braden. Copyright © 1976 Los Angeles *Times.* Reprinted with permission.

Dr Maccoby's article, and *The Executive Life.* Reprinted with permission of *Fortune.*

FIRST EDITION

Designed by Stephanie Krasnow

Library of Congress Cataloging in Publication Data

Boswell, Nelson.
  TA for busy people.

  Includes index.
  1. Success. 2. Transactional analysis. I. Title.
BF637.S8B59 1977   158'.1   77-3738
ISBN 0-06-010427-9

77 78 79 80 10 9 8 7 6 5 4 3 2 1

To Kelly, Nelson, Sean

Contents

Acknowledgments

I wish to express my appreciation to Dr. David Burkhead, psychotherapist, marriage and family counselor, for helping me organize material consisting of early drafts of one third of the book. His friendship, enthusiasm and encouragement will always be remembered.

Ron Van Horn, lecturer, marriage and family counselor using T.A. and Gestalt, donated many hours of his valuable time to read the completed manuscript and made excellent and perceptive suggestions. His warmth, intelligence, and caring for people have earned him an outstanding reputation.

Thanks also go to: Dr. Irving H. Zuckerman who, when we worked together as professors and then administrators at the same university, was a constant source of inspiration; to Dr. Robert G. Talley, our family physician, who took time from a busy schedule to discuss, in specific detail, the appallingly high percentage of patients whose physical illness seemed to originate from mental and emotional stress; to my good friend Hugh Isley who has given freely of his time and expertise; to Nancy Royer for her help in typing the manuscript.

Richard A. Smith and his wife, Barbara, deserve special tribute. Over the years their talents and effort not only have made my syndicated radio program possible, but also have allowed me time to write and research. It's a rare privilege to have such friends.

My colleague and co-worker on the book page by page was Maureen Boswell, my wife. We have worked closely together on many projects in our years of marriage—establishing, writing, and managing my daily radio program; preparing and holding lectures, workshops and seminars; writing books and articles. Her keen insights, creativity and compassionate approach were invaluable to the development of this book, which is her book as well as mine.

Finally, I wish to thank my children—Nelson, Kelly and Sean —whose original viewpoints contributed to the book and who helped every day in so many special ways.

Foreword

Following the hippie revolution in America in the late 1960s, renaissance grass roots movements rose up to offer solutions to the worlds problems. The attitude of complexity and negativity by some seemed balanced by other movements that sought to find the simplicity and positivity in the world. This positive humanistic attitude has grown and influenced the psychological field, with interest developing in TA, gestalt, est, meditation, holistic health, and other growth oriented therapies. Of these, TA is the approach to offer simple positive insights into everyday relationships that may seem negative and complex to us.

In *TA for Busy People,* Nelson Boswell follows the tradition of the TA best sellers *I'm OK—You're OK* and *Born to Win* in presenting TA in a way that is useful and easy to understand. He spans a wide range of TA thinking with simple clarity; he includes current new thinking in TA, and adds a special positive, personal, loving touch that is his own. In his rich use of examples he draws from his own varied background helping people as a man who was college dean, has his own syndicated radio program, is a writer and workshop leader—a background that makes him unique to the field of TA writing.

The book is specific, practical, and helpful. The writing is warm and original, and the message is there for the taking.

1

You Can Apply TA to Your Life Today

A Personal Word to the Reader

Originally this "personal word to the reader" was in a preface, but then I remembered that people sometimes don't read an author's preface and that "busy people," to whom this book is addressed, might be more inclined than the average person to omit the preface and get right down to business. But I want you to read this personal word because it tells you quickly why I wrote this book and what it will do for you. My purpose in the book is to interest you in the exciting possibilities TA (Transactional Analysis) holds for your life, make TA immediately accessible to you, and, most important, show you in simple terms *how to use it.* Huxley was right when he said, "The great end of life is not knowledge, but action." This book, from start to finish, shows you how to put a new knowledge into action in your life.

This is not a psychology textbook, but a guidebook for living and working. It's TA combined with ideas for men and women in active life situations at work and at home, so-called normal people. It's for people who know little or nothing about TA or who have read

1

books on the subject but have not been able to apply it, as well as for those who have already made TA a part of their daily life.

As I was writing this, one of my sons burst into the room with news he had just heard on the radio about a soldier who had been hiding in the jungle for thirty years, not knowing that World War II had ended. "What a terrible waste," said my son. "If only he had known, his life could have been so different." You and I, less dramatically, live in ways we don't have to; we waste our allotted days, not realizing our life could be so different. Like the soldier, we imprison ourselves when freedom and fulfillment are only steps away.

TA can give you that freedom and fulfillment if you know how to use it. It's important for you to know that TA, as I present its application, can help you relax, overcome depression and "down" days, conquer worry, control your anger, communicate better, stop your self-torture, reduce anxiety and stress, handle work situations effectively, get along with others, enliven dating and marriage, enjoy your children, and discover new joy and freedom in your life. With TA you take charge of your life, strengthen and enrich it, and find you have more choices than you thought. As a former professor, accustomed to searching for truth, I dislike making claims; nevertheless, it's true that TA *can* change your life dramatically, and in many ways. TA, a relatively new psychology originated by the late Dr. Eric Berne, a California psychiatrist, is not a fad; you can apply it immediately to the daily problems of living and working once you are shown how.

I want you, before you finish this book, to use TA daily in your life. C. S. Lewis tells about talking with a friend and referring to philosophy as a "subject." His friend replied, "It wasn't a *subject* to Plato; it was a way."* I would like TA to become a "way" for you, a reality in your life, as it has for me, my wife, my children, and those students, mostly working men and women, to whom I

*C. S. Lewis, *Surprised by Joy* (New York: Harcourt, Brace & World, 1955), p. 225.

have taught its application. Not that it will supplant your philosophy or religion; far from it. It will put you in touch with your *self,* make you more tolerant of yourself and others, strengthen your real convictions, and release you to greater joy. TA is a way in that once you have insights into its application, you'll say, "Wow, that's it, that makes sense," and it will become a comfortable, yet pervasive, force in your life.

By the second chapter you will be internalizing TA by seeing its practical use. Although I have given considerable thought to making TA easily understandable in order to get you enthusiastic about its application, I know from past teaching the hazards of oversimplification, where you say "do this" and "do that" and imply that a list from one to ten is all you need to know. Yet many of us remember teachers and professors whose methods were so dry, detailed, and hair-splitting with endless modifications that they turned us off the subject; they guaranteed that once we finished their course we were through forever with what they were teaching. I have long thought that people should first be inspired about something worthwhile, and then they will develop a lifelong curiosity about it. Once you discover the practical use TA has in your life, that it works, you may wish to learn further modifications of the ideas.

There are many short stories about active and busy people, caught in real life situations, in these pages. They will show you quickly that TA is a sensible and practical tool to use in your life. The stories are mostly composites based on actual happenings, but the names, dates, places, times, positions and organizations have all been changed to ensure the privacy of any person, group, or organization. Stories are an interesting and easy way to learn, and you can remember and recall helpful points better if they are presented in that way. The stories are based on facts because, while teaching at four universities, holding workshops, giving speeches around the country, and broadcasting, I've met people who told me stories that are more interesting and illustrate TA points better than anything that could come from imagination alone. There actually was a Mike fired from his job as president of a bank, a woman who ruined her marriage because she couldn't discuss sexual needs with her husband, a Harper who moved from Chicago to Florida three times before he found the life he wanted, a couple who voluntarily moved from a rich to a middle-class neighborhood, a Michelle who felt like a prisoner in her home, a Ralph fired by a drunken vice president, a Margaret and Brian married three years with all their options in life exhausted unless they make a change, an Ann craving affection from her silent husband.

We human beings, you and I, all of us, are difficult to help. If we're successful, we may become arrogant and think no change is necessary, and often, because of this, we become isolated and alone, never fully experience joy, love, or understanding; we become so driven we overreach, or so rigid we destroy our happiness in the end. If, on the other hand, we suffer defeat, we may blame circumstances and think a change in ourselves is useless. TA does not require that you set out to change your personality. As I present it in this book, TA shows you how to understand yourself as you never did before and how to put this knowledge to work in your life so that you experience personal freedom and reach your full human potential.

You Don't Have to "Try Hard"— Just Start Where You Are Now

The chances are there are at least a few things you'd like to change about yourself, even if you're successful. How about that temper that gets away from you, or your down days, or your worry habit, or perhaps the old self-torture game you go through every time you make a mistake, or your inability to really relax and enjoy your accomplishments; maybe you're not being kind enough to yourself, perhaps you treat yourself as an object, something with a market value, and feel you have lost a part of yourself that is very dear to you.

Change has always been very difficult to achieve. Studies conducted on college students when they enter college and again four years later when they leave show that after the expenditure of thousands of dollars and untold effort, their attitudes, opinions, and beliefs have changed very little. Learning psychologists say that for education to have taken place, a behavioral change must have occurred. (In educational terms, behavioral change means a change in either actions or thought processes, or both.) Yet we must sadly conclude that after what is considered the most important educational experience (college), in most cases there has been little, if any, behavioral change in the personality.

Why is it so difficult to change ourselves even in small ways? We have found that positive thinking alone doesn't work for most people because it's too much on the surface. We become inspired to do better but run out of inspirational energy fast, sort of cheer today and gone tomorrow. No behavioral change has taken place. Then, going deeper, we get into Freudian psychoanalysis. Here we're in danger of drowning in morbid and fidgety curiosity about ourselves, awash in jargon and inapplicable ideas. A girl I knew in New York kept a minute-by-minute diary of all her thoughts and reactions during the day and a detailed record of each dream at night. The last I saw her, she was making notes and thinking about herself full-time, totally self-absorbed, with no end in sight.

Most of us are too busy for this. We're in an age of anxiety, living and working under stress, and we simply don't have the time or inclination to make ourselves the subject of a lifelong research program. Transactional Analysis, or TA, does not require this. Dr. Eric Berne coined terms that the layman could understand. His purpose was to help people learn about themselves as quickly as possible. He said that his goal was to cure the patient in the first few minutes of the first session.

Also, TA doesn't call for you to *try hard* to change. In fact, the very phrase "try hard" is anathema to TA practitioners because it shows you are under an internal spell that lessens your happiness and effectiveness. We know the cliché is true that you can't find happiness by searching for it; you become engrossed in something else and then happiness finds you. It's the same in human change; it's psychologically true that to make a change in yourself you don't go about it by making resolutions, gritting your teeth, and forcing it to happen.* You learn about yourself, accept yourself where you are now, and then one day you notice you enjoy yourself and others more, have fewer arguments, handle bad moods better, relax more, enjoy success, and feel more at peace.

This book is not for those who have severe emotional or mental problems, although every day Transactional Analysis is used successfully in therapy by psychiatrists and psychologists to help people who are deeply disturbed. It is also being used successfully by teachers, social workers, clergymen, hospitals, and all kinds of organizations, including billion-dollar companies. TA workshops are held in many cities, and there are several books that go more deeply into TA theory: structural analysis and the analysis of games and scripts. My purpose, however, is to simplify the theoretical and put it on a more practical level. My workshops, seminars, and lectures around the country are mostly for working men and women and their spouses who are busy and under pressure. They need results. I have sometimes been asked to a particular city by the local sponsor of my five-minute syndicated radio program, or by the local radio station on which my program is carried, or a local club or organization. I distill the important points of TA, along with other practical theories, and show these busy people how they can apply it in their daily lives, both at home and at work. I have held workshops or lectured for such diverse groups as managers and administrators, teachers,* personnel managers, un-

---

*Self-contracting or contracting with a therapist or facilitator are effective ways to achieve *specific* changes. It's not effective, for example, to self-contract to become more effective. You can, however, self-contract to read this book twice, or discuss a section each day with a friend, or self-contract for a "Creative Thinking" session twice a week.

*After a speech I gave at a state teachers' convention, I was told the state commissioner was so impressed with the educational possibilities of TA that he was recommending its use by teachers statewide. It is just as useful for business and industry.

dergraduate and graduate students, firefighters, Sales and Marketing Executives clubs, secretaries, housewives, and others; TA can be applied in all these special situations.

In the following chapters, we'll be referring to your three selves. The theory of Transactional Analysis holds that you are three people in one; you have three entirely different behavior modes in which you operate. The three selves within you were first recognized and classified by Dr. Eric Berne. They were verified by his studies and reconfirmed by thousands of psychologists, psychiatrists, counselors, and other therapists.

Dr. Berne called these three entirely different ways in which we human beings operate "ego states." This is not just a clever idea, but an observable reality. He said we each have a Parent ego state, an Adult ego state, and a Child ego state. *Parent, Adult, and Child, when capitalized, refer to ego states and not to persons.* Incidentally, these three ego states are not the same as Freud's ego, id, and superego. No one has ever seen an "id" or "superego," but right from the start in these pages, you'll recognize and observe your three ego states and how they affect your life.

An old friend of mine from New York, whom I had not seen for many years, called me last week to let me know he was in town, and we had dinner together. I was surprised to see that he still chain-smoked, drank too much and overate, although he had suffered a severe heart attack. I had originally treasured his friendship for various reasons, but his conversation, as we ate dinner, was dotted with numbers and status symbols: his income, tax bracket, square feet in his house, accountant's fee, cost of car, kids' tuition at the "best" school. He sounded as if he were outside himself, no longer in touch with his inner core, but merely estimating his market value with an accumulation of statistics. My friend seemed locked into a joyless and impractical pattern of thought and behavior that might very well end his life prematurely.

I mentioned to him I was working on a book that would make a powerful new psychological tool, TA, immediately usable in a person's life. "Yeah, yeah, yeah," he said hurriedly, "I know all about that. It's Parent, Adult, Child. Great stuff."

My friend's comment reminded me of the speed-reading expert who said, after reading Tolstoy's monumental *War And Peace* in just half an hour, "It's about Russia." We summarize something and miss its meaning. I don't want you to do this with TA. It's an exciting and profound new psychology; it is "great stuff," but only if we, unlike my friend, know how to use it in our lives.

2

Your Controlling
Tape Collection

When we're in our Parent ego state, we operate from preprogrammed information. This information is stored in our brain like
a huge tape collection. Dr. Thomas Harris says: "The Parent is a
huge collection of recordings in the brain of unquestioned or im-
posed external events perceived by a person in his early years.
. . . In the Parent are recorded all the admonitions and rules and
laws that the child heard from his parents and saw in their living."*
James and Jongeward say: "The Parent ego state contains the
attitudes and behavior incorporated from external sources, primarily parents. Outwardly, it often is expressed toward others in preju-
dicial, critical, and nurturing behavior. Inwardly, it is experienced
as old Parental messages which continue to influence the inner
Child."†

When someone says something to us, or something happens and
we set ourselves off, our thoughts or words come rushing down a

*Thomas A. Harris, *I'm OK—You're OK,* (New York: Harper & Row, 1967),
pp. 40 and 42, Avon Edition.
†M. James and D. Jongeward, *Born to Win* (Reading, Mass.: Addison-Wesley
Publishing Co., 1971), p. 17.

preformed pathway. One way of picturing what happens is to imagine an amusement park ride that takes you down a long metal chute into the water. Once the lever at the top is pulled, the boat races down the chute. That lever and that boat represent the way we respond in the Parent ego state. Once a "lever" is pulled in our environment, this stimulus activates the Parent tapes. It should encourage you to know that with the information I'm going to give you, you can, if you find it desirable, learn to slow that boat down or divert it. Those pathways will always exist, but we can learn to control what goes down them.

The thousands and thousands of messages in our brain are called "Parent" tapes because they have been programmed in us by our parents and other significant figures in our early life. When we are in the Parent ego state, we are acting, talking, and "thinking" like our parents. "Thinking" is in quotes because when we're in the Parent ego state, we only think we're thinking. (There are several exceptions to this statement, which need not concern us at this time.)

Many of these Parent tapes help us all our lives and are essential for our survival. They play softly, like Muzak, in the background, barely perceptible; with our hardly being aware, they get us up on time, bathed and starting our day's work. The beneficial tapes keep us from injuring others when we're angry, lighting a match to see how full the gas tank is, snatching a watch from the department store counter. They also soothe us, help us care about ourselves as human beings.

There are thousands of these helpful messages stored in our brain that automatically protect us, and they are there because someone cared enough to tell us what they thought we should know. Our parents were the best parents they knew how to be. But there, of course, is the rub. While they were doing perhaps the best they could, they may have made mistakes, minor or major ones, and some of the Parent tapes they passed on to us may be very harmful, even though they may not have meant them to be. It depends on how they perceived the world they lived in, and this was determined by the Parent tapes they inherited, how they felt about themselves and others, and such events as wars, depressions, job loss, divorce, sickness. Whatever the mistakes your parents might have made, sooner or later, as you take charge of your life, you'll want to forgive them, the same as you'll want to forgive your own mistakes; and it may help you if you remember that not too many years ago there were few guidelines for parents, and few of them had the leisure to think about them anyway.

The Nurturing Parent Ego State

One part of the Parent ego state helps people learn and grow. It's called the Nurturing Parent and consists of all the love, supportiveness, and encouragement that we experienced early in life. There is a negative side to the Nurturing Parent, which is inauthentic or inappropriately helpful ("I'll do your homework for you," "You'd better let me do that job for you," etc.), but from now on when I refer to the Nurturing Parent, I mean the helpful part only. Our Nurturing Parent ego state allows us to be kind to ourselves and kind to others. When we are in our Nurturing Parent, we can feel for others, communicate with them, and set a climate in which they can talk to us. The Nurturing Parent makes statements (and plays tapes) that encourage. When we nurture ourselves, we give ourselves permission to experiment without fear of failure, take personal risks for growth, experience setbacks without quitting. We are kind and gentle with ourselves, and then we are nurturing and helpful to others.

The Critical Parent Ego State

The Critical Parent ego state has a positive side, which includes the controlling advice necessary to the preservation of health and well-being, but from now on when I refer to the Critical Parent, I'm talking about the harmful part.

When we're in our Critical Parent ego state, we cause misery to ourselves and others. The Critical Parent talks to us (we talk to ourselves) and finds fault. It is unreasonable, unloving, and it destroys our peace of mind. When the Critical Parent is driving a person, he* will be out of touch with reality and defeat his own objectives. A person driven by Critical Parent tapes becomes alienated from his real self. If he follows the tapes blindly, he is a living robot, preprogrammed with what to do, what to think, what to say, and what to be. There is no real person left. People with strong prerecorded statements and feelings, bearing little relationship to reality, have caused great tragedies throughout history—from the Inquisition, to Hitler's Germany, to the all-out attack today on man's faith in God and the meaningfulness of life. Prejudice is, of course, prerecorded. The authoritarian, opinionated, prejudiced person is operating on Critical Parent tapes much of the time. He's often wrong, but seldom in doubt.

On a personal level, the Critical Parent tapes destroy relationships, establish a tense and unhappy atmosphere in the home and at work, and when we turn the Critical tapes against ourselves, they cause us to feel depressed, guilty, angry, sad, or lonely. People on Critical Parent tapes may tell you how to raise children, although they have never had any. They can tell you what to do in the stock market right after they have lost a bundle. On a moment's notice they can give career counseling, psychotherapy, economic advice, or tell you what's wrong with the country today. People in the Critical Parent ego state are not interested in the here and now, life itself, the substance of anything. The Critical Parent is interested in form only, whether the person is feeling enough stress, whether there is a great enough feeling of trying hard, rushing, pleasing, meeting schedules.

---

*I considered alternating pronouns throughout the book, one time "she" the next "he," but this diverts the reader's mind. Someday I hope there will be a solution to this language problem that forces writers to treat men and women unequally.

How the Tapes Control You

What happens when the Critical Parent voice drives a person, controlling his words and actions? Since many people operate on Parent tapes, examples abound:

A teacher on Parent tapes to maintain strict discipline spends her time keeping her class quiet, neat, and solemn. She is much more interested in discipline at the drinking fountain than in the amount of learning that takes place in the children. Her students find her so dull, unrealistic, and threatening, the only thing they learn is to hate school.

The president of a small organization under the Parental command to try harder and harder never feels he is doing well enough. He is unmerciful to himself. His business is prospering, but he doesn't feel successful. He drives himself relentlessly and seeks perfection even in his relaxation. His Critical Parent may drive him to an early death. This type can spend a lifetime pursuing the future and never once experience the "here and now." He doesn't even know what the here and now really *feels* like.

A housewife driven by tapes that tell her she must be perfect tries to be the ideal mother, wife, cook, hostess, companion, and lover. She never feels satisfied with herself, never knows peace of mind.

The nurse on tapes demanding punctuality wakes her patient to give him a sleeping pill. The restaurant owner under the Parental command to be orderly becomes so obsessed with details he completely forgets the comfort and enjoyment of his patrons.

The Parental inner messages whip us to greater and greater effort with never a moment to relax. But the effort we exert is not toward a realistic objective. The man or woman on Parent tapes often repeats himself over and over. You sometimes get a feeling of unreality talking to such people because they don't respond to what you say. If you try to agree with them, their Critical tapes may override your agreement and you find yourself once again on the wrong side of them.

People on Parent tapes are like one-way radios; they only transmit. They have no receiving mode, nothing comes through to them. They absorb little from their environment. Reality to them is the Critical and controlling tapes in their head that play on and on. When the Critical tapes become your reality, you lose touch with your spouse, children, friends, and associates. You truly become an *alien* to the situation you're in, whether at work or in your home life. Let's look briefly at two situations, one in the home with a husband and wife, and one in the office with a sales manager.

Warren Says It's OK, but Michelle's Tapes Won't Let Her

Michelle and Warren, both in their thirties, have a problem threatening their marriage which Michelle thought would solve itself when all her children were in school. When the children were small and still at home, Michelle felt down and depressed many days. She felt completely isolated from the rest of the world. Even though she loved them, she resented the unending attention they required, but she never mentioned her problem to anyone.

Michelle's problem didn't end when all the children finally went off to school. She still finds her life boring, repetitive, and unchallenging. She tries to keep the house spotless, be a loving wife and mother, be Michelle-on-the-spot for her husband; she loves her family very much. But she still suffers periods of depression and wonders: "Is this all there is to life?"

Michelle brought up her problem at a workshop she attended with Warren. Another woman at the workshop said the same problem was the reason for her divorce. "My husband wouldn't let me work," she said, "and it got so I couldn't stand the daily routine inside the house all day."

"Why won't you let Michelle get a job?" one of the single girls asked Warren. It came out later that this girl, a pediatric nurse, had recently broken up with her boyfriend because she was afraid of the possible suffocating effect of marriage. Warren, who seemed to be an easy going person, smiled at this question and said, "We've talked about a lot of things together, but this is the first I've heard that Michelle was bored at home."

Michelle felt too guilty to discuss it with Warren. Here she was with everything that she had always been told, both by parents and by society, a girl could wish for—loving husband, healthy children, comfortable home, security; and yet she, wretched creature that she thought she was, was not appreciative. So her Critical tapes beat down on her, telling her she was a poor excuse for a woman and not to bother her hard-working husband with such nonsense.

I think it's important to insert a note here about playing our own tapes when we read this story. If your tapes are the same as Michelle's, then you'll have no sympathy for her, just as she has none for herself. "She's lucky she has a fine husband who is willing to take care of her," you may think. You'd be partially right, and Michelle would agree with you and continue feeling more unhappy each day. But it's good to look at these problems in a clinical way, in our Adult, to help ourselves and others solve them.

Michelle had been raised by a loving mother and father, who taught her, because they believed it and it worked for them:

"A good husband provides the living."

"A woman's place is in the home."

"A good wife and mother is always available to her husband and children."

"Careers are not for women."

"It is wrong for a woman to want more than a husband, children, and a good home."

Many men and women find happiness and the life they were seeking with the husband working and the wife spending full time at home; for other couples this doesn't work. Sometimes it isn't practical. As the cost of living goes up, many couples want or need the extra income from the wife's job. Other couples find that the wife's working adds zest to their lives.

The important thing is that each person in the marriage be aware
of his real needs, communicate these needs fully to his partner, and
then strive wholeheartedly to satisfy his own and each other's
needs. Over the years, as they change and grow, their needs and
wishes may change, and for continuing fulfillment they will perhaps want to redefine their original marriage commitment. (See
Chapter 11: Freedom in Marriage.)

Michelle and Warren were able to solve their problem, as was
the single girl who feared the restrictions of marriage, after learning how to get in touch with themselves and with their loved ones
through TA. Methods to accomplish this are in the following
chapters.

Why Jim Can't Manage

Jim was a single man and his problem was not in his home life,
but at work. He was sales manager for the electrical appliances
division of a large company in the Midwest. He performed well
after he received his promotion to sales manager, as long as the
product was selling well. However, when the competition came out
with a product which it promoted aggressively and sold with zeal,
Jim was at a loss to meet this challenge. From the very first sales
meeting Jim held, until the last meeting before he lost his job, he
was operating on tapes, and so was his secretary. Whenever Jim
talked with his salesmen, whether in a meeting or individually, it
was as if Jim had been preprogrammed with what to say. He was
trapped by the role he thought he should play.

Who knows where Jim picked up the information stored in his
head about how a sales manager should think, act, talk, and manage? Some tapes came from his childhood, from his authoritarian
father. Some were stored in his head later; perhaps it was at some
highly theoretical business school, or maybe he had seen too many
grade B movies in which the executive was aggressive, decisive,
quick-thinking, abrupt, dynamic, intimidating, and unapproach-

able. Whatever the source, Jim had messages going through his head which said:

"Real executives make quick decisions."

"A leader never shows doubt."

"People lose respect for you if you tell them you had not thought of the idea they presented."

"People need to be forced to work."

"You motivate people by telling them to work harder."

"Managers must do more talking than listening."

"Strong executives don't ask questions; they give orders."

And then, on top of the handicap of these inaccurate messages, Jim's Critical Parent tapes were triggered whenever people didn't do things the way he thought they should. Never mind that one of his top salesmen worked hard and effectively; the man didn't turn in his reports on time and they were sloppy and incomplete. As Jim's secretary said (she had an inner Critical Parent voice telling her the only worthwhile goal was getting things neat and orderly): "Sure, I know he's the top salesman, but that's no excuse for getting the reports in late. You'll simply have to crack down on him. You can't make exceptions."

Jim agreed with his secretary. He didn't realize she was operating from her Critical Parent ego state and suggesting that Jim "raise" his salesmen much the same way she had raised her children. So with old, memorized opinions on how people should be managed, Jim tried to run a sales organization. He called meetings and did most of the talking. He laid down the law and told everyone they had to work harder. He demanded creative selling without once thinking what this meant. He went through the motions of soliciting ideas from his sales force, but the climate he set discouraged feedback totally.

Consequently, Jim received little information from those working for him, and became more and more separated from reality as time passed. If the buyer for a large department store told the top salesman they had received a better advertising allowance from

Competitor A, this information was not passed on to Jim. The salesman knew Jim would give him some memorized pap such as: "That's negative thinking" or "You're not trying hard enough." The feeling among the salesmen became: "We'll give the S.O.B. just what he and his 'assistant sales manager' [Jim's secretary] want— and that's neat reports." And since any good salesman knows that sales managers like Jim come and go, they decided to wait until a new manager was put in charge.

How to Tell if You're Under a Spell

There are many people like Michelle and Jim, men and women whose lives are acted out according to memorized statements that they have never examined. Some of these people cannot help themselves without the aid of a trained TA therapist because one of the commands implanted in their brain is: "Don't think about yourself." Others of us can tune in on the controlling inner voice, although this is not easy because we must, in effect, use our mind to examine our mind. One thing we must avoid is the attitude: "That's just the way I am. I'm the worrying kind" or "I've got an ungovernable temper and that's all there is to it." There are many behavioral characteristics that signify you are under the spell of the Critical inner voice. Here are a few:

> You worry most of the time.
> You don't relax, take a vacation, let down, take a day off and *let go.*
> You won't give a sucker an even break; you insist on a pound of flesh.
> You string together meaningless clichés in place of thinking.
> You feel behind in your work; you are usually in a hurry. (The Critical Parent is not satisfied with how much you accomplish each day.)
> You berate yourself for imperfections.
> You feel: "What's the use of trying?" (The Critical Parent will be displeased anyway.)

You're successful, but don't enjoy it; or successful, but feel like
a failure.

You often experience inappropriate feelings of anger, hurt,
fear, or inadequacy.

You don't feel a healthy concern for yourself as a struggling
human being doing the best you can.

Inner Commands* That Determine Your Life

To help you identify some of the recorded messages in your
brain, I have listed below a few of the inner commands that are
easily recognized. These inner commands restrict your life, narrow
personal freedom, and destroy openness and spontaneity. I think
you'll find some of the messages familiar, and they'll help you hear
your own Critical Parent tapes.

"If you want something done right, you have to do it yourself."

Thousands of people limit their potential by refusing to delegate
responsibility to others. One of my students, a production engineer
studying for his master's degree, told me that time after time he
fails to turn over even simple jobs to his subordinates, and then
always feels hurried because he does not only his job, but the jobs
of those working for him. He said he recently missed a promotion
and thought it might be because he had no one ready for his
position if he moved up.

"You made your bed; now lie in it."

This message severely limits problem-solving ability. One man
in his late twenties had been selling insurance for three years. It was
the wrong kind of work for him. He didn't like it and wasn't doing
well, but he had a tape in his head telling him he had chosen the
wrong occupation and now he must live with that mistake. After

*Keep in mind that these are not always verbal.

he identified this harmful inner command, he was able to free his Adult ego state, assess the reality of his situation, and take steps to improve it. Today he is a happy and successful professor at a large Southern university. He found his niche, as his students would tell you; they voted him Teacher of the Year.

Another student, a young woman, was able to make a dramatic change in her life after recognizing this same tape. She had eloped when she was eighteen. Her football hero turned out to be a disastrous husband; he drank heavily and beat her. She believed the inner voice that told her this is what you get for marrying so young. When her Adult was able to take over, she sought legal advice on her problem. The marriage was terminated and she has a new start.

"Don't act big."

In England the direction of a person's life is determined early and he may find himself labeled "working class" at a very young age. Many in the United States do not take advantage of the freedom they have to attempt upward mobility. The inner voice says to them, "Who do you think you are, trying to be somebody? Give up. Stay where you belong."

"You're laughing now, but you'll soon be crying."

This tape is identified most often by students in their forties and fifties. Several recalled their childhood days during the Depression when their fathers would say, "Well, there's food on the table today, but we may soon be going hungry." The feeling they got was that they shouuldn't be too pleased if things were going well at the moment because it wasn't going to last long. One man said, "To this day it's difficult for me to let go and enjoy myself for fear it will bring me bad luck, sort of 'Laugh now and pay later.' We learned in my family you ward off disaster by not allowing yourself to be too happy."

"Be serious."

Many people have been raised to be serious, quiet, and dignified at all times. Any laughter, shouting, and horseplay was swiftly punished. A poignant example in one group was a middle-aged woman. She has an important administrative position in the public school system. She's a hard worker and a great asset to her community. She is also quiet, controlled, serious, and dignified.

One evening when we were discussing this inner command, Eva said she had become aware of how that voice ruled her life and robbed her of fun. At that moment something humorous happened. I've forgotten now what it was, but Eva laughed. She laughed the same way she always did, but this was the first time she realized that every time she laughed she put her head down and covered her face with her hand. Her inner command "Be serious" forced her to hide herself when she laughed.

Another consequence of the "Be serious" command is that many people cannot allow their own children to laugh and cut up at home. And if they want to have fun themselves they have to go out, get away from the home atmosphere before they can allow their Child freedom to have a good time.

"Never play until all your work is done."

Obeying this inner voice puts people in bondage for life. As one man said, "I have my own business and there is always something I can be doing in connection with it. This means I can never relax. The minute I want to have some fun, something tells me I'd better not because there's some work I could be doing." This inner command also destroys the happiness of many a housewife. It is literally true that a wife or mother without household help—and very few can afford help today—seldom gets caught up.

"People should always get along with each other."

A woman with this inner message told the group that it drives her right up the wall when her children fight with each other. "I really suffer when they fight," she said, "and the result is that in breaking up their fight, I scream and shout louder and longer than they did."

"You never do things right."

One middle-aged student said that her mother always complained about the mess she made when she was learning to cook. Her mother would say, "You're all thumbs. Let me do it before you spill it." She says she still can't cook and feels like a bungler, not only in the kitchen, but in everything else she does.

"Always do what is expected of you."

People who live under this spell have lost their freedom and autonomy. They may find themselves in the wrong career or married to the wrong person. A housewife under the spell of this command must please each child, her husband, her husband's boss, the neighbors, the neighbors' children, and the children's teachers. She must be Suzie Eveready, satisfying every desire and expectation of everyone she comes in contact with.

"You must be respectable."

This inner message is especially damaging. Those who guide their lives by this command can spend a lifetime seeking the approval of others. The approval sought can be from the "cultured," the "intellectuals," or "society." The person shifts his center of being from himself to others, striving to own the "right" house, serve the "right" wine, and drive the "right" car.

"You must be liked."

This command is similar to "You must be respectable" and causes great human misery. Some people have been raised by parents who required that they be popular. The parents insisted that their children get along and be liked by everyone, and then wondered why they succumbed to peer group pressure to experiment with drugs; or why their daughter, so the most popular boy in her class would like her, got pregnant in the back seat of his car.

The truth of the matter is that, psychologically speaking, you should, by the time you reach middle age, have several real friends (probably three or four is plenty) so that you have healthy transactions with other human beings and don't exist in an isolated world. But other than that, the old navy expression still remains true: "You only need six for pallbearers."

The Child within us has a natural tendency to want to get along because it seems to many of us to be the safest way to cope. The Adult within, instead of reinforcing this tendency of the Child to crave the approval of everyone, should lean against the tendency and tell the Child it's OK to be yourself.

William H. Holloway, M.D., and Martha M. Holloway say in their pamphlet, "Change Now": "We struggle to please, struggle to get ahead, struggle to earn bread, struggle to be accepted by others or God, we even struggle to find time to relax. When life is such a struggle, there is little joy and intimacy and one does not feel in charge of one's self. We seem always to be meeting the expectations of others or the standards someone set for us as a child and we now demand of ourselves.

"With all those struggles we begin to live as though our life was at stake with every act, every decision, every thought at every moment. *You don't have to do that to yourself.*"*

---

*"Change Now!" An Introduction to Contractual Group Treatment with Transactional Analysis, William H. Holloway, M.D. and Martha M. Holloway. Copyright 1973 William H. Holloway. Permission granted the author in a conversation with William H. Holloway, M.D., President, International Transactional Analysis Association.

It's not easy to get in touch with your Parent ego state, but it's not impossible either; and it's always worth the effort. The following ideas will help you do it.

How to Get in Touch with Your Parent Ego State

1. Recall several statements you make that you remember your parents making.

2. Ask yourself what you say when you're angry. How do you look? Do you behave and look as your parents did when they were angry? Are your statements, when angry, recorded messages?

3. Review the clichés you use. Catch yourself using them. Are they really true and the result of reasoning in the present, or are they recorded announcements?

4. Ask yourself if you generalize life so that everything, every person, and every group is categorized and labeled? Are you able to make fine differentiations?

5. Ask a member of your family to tell you when you have shifted from a reasoning Adult to Critical tapes. Discuss specifically what you say and what triggers it.

6. In your work and at home do you exercise authority merely because you have it? Ask yourself what rules, regulations, and forms *really* contribute and which are simply to control the actions of others.

7. Check your awareness by asking yourself how often you admit you're wrong. Give yourself no credit for statements like: "I know I make mistakes at times," "I'm only human," and "I've been wrong before." These are recorded statements used by persons who very seldom admit specific error in the here and now.

8. Do you use these or similar recorded announcements:

"There's no doubt about it."
"People don't want to work anymore."
"I'm doing this for the good of the organization."
"You can't trust anyone."

"I'm always fair."

"When I say something, I mean it."

9. The Nurturing Parent ego state encourages people. How often do you say:

"That was a fine job."

"Thanks for the extra effort."

"Jim, you seem upset. What can I do to help?"

"I know exactly how you feel. I made a bigger mistake last week."

"You help our organization [family] very much. I don't even like to consider what we would do without you."

10. Ask yourself how you feel about the following subjects:

Sex
Money
Education
Career
Religion
Children
Approval of others
Men's and women's roles

Review each subject separately. Can you talk about each item openly? Are you uncomfortable when you think about one of them? Do you have statements about any of the subjects that you hear yourself saying? Are your feelings and opinions about these subjects the same as your parents'?

11. What were the three most important values to your parents? List them. What are your most important values? Are they the same, similar, or totally different? Are they the same or similar because you are conforming, or totally different because you are rebelling? Can you be comfortable examining them and coming to your own conclusions?

12. As you go about your daily routine, ask yourself at every

opportunity what your parents would have said and how they would have acted in the same situation. Are you doing what they would have done? Is there anything about your behavior you want to change?

13. When you say or think the words "should" or "ought," ask yourself if these are Parent tapes you're playing. Examine the "should" or "ought" to see if it is really true and life-giving. Does it lead to happiness and fulfillment?

14. Take notice when you say "never," "always," "for sure," "I'm positive." Did your parents use the same words? About the same subjects?

15. Some people tell me they feel uneasy examining their Parent tapes. They feel disloyal to their parents. However, they soon discover there are many parent tapes they want to keep, and only a few must be discarded. One man found he was as much under a spell rebelling against the Parent tapes in his head as another person who conforms blindly to them. Neither way is free, of course. After you review your Parent tapes, you may very well feel closer to your parents, living or dead. When you can look at your parents as two very human people, capable of making mistakes, just as you are, you have taken a step toward freedom. You have also taken a step toward loving them in a realistic way.

3

Discovering the Power
of Your Adult Ego State

When we're in our Adult ego state, we're like a computer; we collect data, test reality, consider alternatives and options, assess probabilities, and deal objectively with the problem at hand.

Think about the Adult ego state of a commercial jet pilot, and you'll get a good idea how yours and mine should work. The pilot keeps finely attuned to the reality around him: weather, attitude, altitude, fuel level, consumption rate, distances, airspeed, and a hundred other things that tell him precisely what is going on inside and outside the plane. He makes adjustments in accordance with what he sees. He doesn't use outdated maps (Critical Parent), nor, if confronted with foul weather, does he run down the aisle shouting, "This is terrible, I can't stand it. I give up" (fearful Child). (The Child ego state is explained in Chapter 4.) Dr. Thomas Harris says: "One of the important functions of the Adult is to examine the data in the Parent, to see whether or not it is true and still applicable today, and then to accept it or reject it, and to examine the Child to see whether or not the feelings there are appropriate to the present or are archaic and in response to archaic Parent data. The goal is not to do away with the Parent and

27

Child but to be free to examine these bodies of data."*

Our Adult ego state, like that of the jet pilot, helps us survive and makes it possible for us to get where we want to go. Remember the pilot when you're immobilized with inappropriate Child feelings or listening to Critical Parent tapes that are not quite accurate. From the comparison with the pilot, you can also see that the fully functioning Adult ego state has the following characteristics:

> It is fact-finding.
> It is objective.
> It assesses probabilities and possibilities.
> It weighs risks and rewards.
> It tests reality.
> It can hold conflicting data in mind.
> It free wheels like radar, searching out further clues.
> It makes fine discriminations.
> It is goal-seeking.

The Adult as Executive of the Personality

The Adult ego state, of course, is only as good as the information it takes in and understands. The pilot, to function, must know about flying; and the human being, to become fully functioning, must have an accurate idea of how things work in his world. To be fully functioning requires a delicate balance. The Adult ego should not be contaminated with unexamined prejudiced Parent information or archaic Child feelings; yet, at the same time, the personality must have at its disposal all three ego states so that there is not an exclusion of Child feelings, nor an absence of Parental information.

William James said years ago that "A great many people think they are thinking when they are merely rearranging their prejudices." We're all guilty of this at times, some of us more than

---

*I'm OK—You're OK; Avon edition, p. 53.

others. When I taught, I spent considerable time trying to figure a way to cut through the prejudices, preconceptions, and hardened archaic ideas to the minds of the students. It was obvious that James was right, that many of them refused to think, use their Adult ego state, and merely played a combination of old, outdated tapes, tapes that many of these men and women could combine into what passed as thinking. I never found a way that satisfied me completely to break through to and activate the Adult ego state, free it, and enable it to function fully and precisely. I think perhaps other professors have, but at best it's a difficult undertaking. Those who teach at universities and colleges without prestige, where the problem is to get enough students every year, have an almost impossible task. If they push their students hard to rid them of their prejudices and get them to operate in their Adult, they may very well frighten and anger them. If that happens, the professor will lose his popularity, and the chances are, at a student-hungry school, the professor who shakes the students up too much will be let go.*

You must not believe here, when I'm talking about prejudices, that I'm referring to man's faith. I believe faith is necessary to a human being. Intrinsic faith does not come under the heading of prejudice. Real faith is a commitment made by the Adult in conjunction with the Child. The Adult examines the Parent tapes—perhaps the religion he was taught as a child—decides he believes the core of what he was taught, and commits his life to it. Prejudice, to me, would be not respecting the rights of others to go their own way after you had made your commitment.

I said a moment ago that during a teaching career I did not find

*A step toward getting people to use their Adult more effectively would be to teach them the principles of TA when they are young. As a former educator, I know such a sensible program would yield practical results, both in mental health and in student self-realization. It would be a simple program to set up in connection with qualified local TA therapists and would be nonthreatening to any of the present curricula.

a way that satisfied me completely to free the Adult in students for objective computing. This concerns me, too, a little about what I'm writing here. You can have so much freedom if you put your Adult in charge of your personality, but I don't know if mere words will get you to do this. I hope so. But you see, the trick is to catch yourself on the wing. It's you who must decide to get in touch with yourself. It's you who must not only read what I'm saying, but somehow internalize it and then use your mind to "spy" on yourself. It's a fine point, but one with such potential. Please think about it a little because what I'm discussing strikes at the very heart of living a full life.

When you start thinking about putting your Adult in charge of your personality, exciting ideas come to mind. Your Adult can be made powerful, you can use it to get the very most the circumstances of your life allow, and yes, even use it to change some of those circumstances. You can also use it so that other people can't hurt you.

The Adult Protects the Child

You can make your Adult powerful enough that, as the executive of your personality, it protects your Child from all negative strokes, whether from strangers, loved ones, or whomever. You see, when someone hands us a downer, we can, if we don't know better, grab it with our Child ego state, hug it to ourselves, and rock back and forth, locked into our practiced negative feeling. But we don't have to do this. It's our choice. The Adult in charge of the personality says, in effect, "Buster, you are responsible for your feelings, and I am responsible for mine, and I *choose* to reject that downer you handed me and let it fly away on the wind. If you don't like me, mister, and you find my person objectionable, then that is a problem you have." The powerful Adult can look at a barb headed for his Child and say, "That has no value at all to my personality," and discard it. (See "Your Defense Against Negative Strokes" in Chapter 5.)

There's also the reverse of this coin. The Adult decides that others are responsible for their feelings. If their date, or spouse, or teen-ager *chooses* (and that is actually what happens, they choose) to be irritable, mean, or depressed, then the Adult says, in effect, "I'm sorry you choose to feel that way. I can offer you my help, I can offer you my sympathy, but I am not responsible for your feelings. They are your feelings and *you* own them, and I choose not to join you in feeling bad."

The Powerful Adult Goes Straight and Stays Out of the Rackets

The Adult decides to take charge of his feelings and stay out of "racket feelings"—one of the many ideas of Eric Berne that give people deep insight into themselves. Berne said the racket feelings are "chiefly guilt, fear, hurt, anger, and often inadequacy, stupidity, or bafflement as well."* As children we experimented with different feelings and found that certain ones were forbidden by our family, and others were encouraged. Some families encourage the "let's get with it and solve our problems" type behavior, and other families teach the child nonproductive feelings so that when things go wrong, or he becomes frustrated, he sinks into a feeling that makes his problem even worse. The child then practices these nonproductive feelings, finds one that he favors more than others, this becomes to him the usual way to react to a situation, and he becomes as automatic in turning on this feeling as the actor in a Broadway production may become in his lines.

It will be difficult, perhaps, for your Adult to get in touch with your racket feeling. The reason, of course, is that you may very well

*E. Berne, *Principles of Group Treatment* (New York: Grove Press, 1966), p. 286.

consider that when you get angry at your date, or spouse, or children, just for example, there is no other possible reaction you could have. After all, you say, they were in the wrong. Naturally, this is incorrect; it's not the only reaction you could have. I have found that one way to get in touch with your racket feeling is to ask yourself, when you find yourself flooded with a particular feeling, one simple question: How is this feeling helping me to get on with my life? If the feeling is not helping you get on with the business of living, then it really isn't authentic, is it? In other words, you might call it just a little bit dishonest, sort of a racket *you* allow yourself to practice.

Sometimes a person "likes" his favored racket feeling of anger, hurt, guilt, etc., so much that he collects these feelings, stores them up, and then turns them in for a "free prize." In TA terms this is known as stamp collecting. Here are examples of stamps that a person might collect, together with the kind of prize they might be turned in for:

Name of Stamp	Life Position	Color	Can Be Redeemed For:	
			Small Prize	Large Prize
Anger	You're Not OK	Red	Tell someone off	Homicide
Inadequacy	I'm Not OK	Gray	Drop course	Quit school
Guilt	I'm Not OK	Brown	Consistently late for work	Fired from job
Depression	I'm Not OK	Blue	Collapse for day	Suicide

The Karpman* Drama Triangle

Many people get an immediate insight into their behavior and the behavior of others with the Karpman Drama Triangle:

*Permission granted by Stephen B. Karpman, M.D.

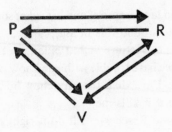

In the Drama Triangle there are three roles the players may take, and they represent the illegitimate escalation of favorite bad feelings. The player can begin at any point and be assured he'll get to play each of the three roles.

The Persecutor. In the Drama Triangle, the Persecutor may be unnecessarily strict, controlling or angry for the purpose of provoking a certain response from another player.

The Rescuer. The person who is the Rescuer in the Drama Triangle inappropriately rescues someone who does not need rescuing. He "saves" someone needlessly. He intrudes where he has no business.

The Victim. The Victim in the Drama Triangle feels hurt, put upon and powerless when in reality there is a simple solution to his problem. He is the Victim, not as someone who is criminally attacked is a victim, but because he *chooses* to be a victim.

Let's take an example of the Karpman Drama Triangle:

Dad (as Persecutor, to son): "Why the hell didn't you mow the lawn like you're supposed to? That's the least you could do.

Son (as Victim): "I have to do all the dirty work. Why always pick on me? It's a terrible job."

Mom (as Rescuer): "He hasn't been feeling well, and he has all that homework. I told him to take it easy." (She switches to Persecutor of father): "You're always picking on him. Why don't you mow the damned lawn yourself and get rid of some of that fat. You do precious little around this house."

Dad (switches to Victim): "Oh, I'm fat, am I? I'll bet my repulsiveness is why we have trouble with you know what. Nobody cares about my heart. I'm exhausted, my chest hurts, but I'll mow it myself. So what if it kills me."

Son (switches to Rescuer): "I'll do it right now, Dad. I know you're tired. Let me get you a drink." (switches to Persecutor of Mom): "It's Mom's fault; she told me I didn't have to do it."

Mom (switches to Victim): "Oh, sure, it's my fault. Anything that goes wrong around here is always blamed on me."

And on they go, racing around the triangle, switching roles. Can you see the endless possibilities for such relationships between people, both in the home and at work? Good triangle players can go from home to filling station to office to night-school, to the grocery store or the theatre and find Drama Triangle action. It's not hard to find others who are willing and able to play.

Go For The Good Feelings

Are there options to the ersatz living that takes place in the triangle? Of course there are, and you can probably think of them yourself. Remember the football adage that says the guy with the ball should run for daylight; this sort of applies to the triangle. Make it a practice in your life to break out of the triangle and "go for the good feelings." There are times when you may be legitimately angry, but you don't have to turn it into a drama.

Here's one way that family dialogue could have gone if everyone came on straight:

Dad: "Son, the grass-cutting is overdue. No hassle, but two more days and it'll cost you two dollars from your allowance (or the use of the car, etc.)." (Then, going for the good feelings, he might say something like, "Would you like to go to the movie with your mother and me tonight?")

Mom: "You two settle the grass problem. I've got other fish to fry."

Son: "Dad, it's been heavy at school this week. I've got studying to do today. I'll do the grass tomorrow."

The Powerful Adult Generally Is in Charge Of:

1. Monitoring the Parent tapes, considering past advice, opinion, earlier education, etc., to see if they're applicable to the present.

2. Turning the volume down on harsh Critical Parent tapes, protecting the Child from self-destructive messages.

3. Activating the Nurturing Parent tapes when appropriate to encourage the Child in working toward a goal or when things go wrong.

4. Keeping in touch with the feelings of the Child, allowing the OK Child to have fun, and holding the Not OK Child in check.

5. Considering the ethics involved in a situation.

6. Integrating all three ego states so that the person can live and work up to his full potential as a human being.

The Powerful Adult Also:

Sets Realistic Goals

It is the Child ego state that says, "I'm going to write a book" or "I'm going to be top salesman" or "I'm going to get an advanced degree," and then does nothing about it. It is the Adult that sets achievable and realistic goals and then takes steps to reach them. (See Chapter 10: What It Really Takes to Succeed.) The Adult sets a goal of writing one page, or making one call, or registering for one course *today*.

Knows There's a Lot of Missing in Winning

The Child *expects* everything to go right, the Critical Parent may *demand* that everything go right, but it is the Adult that knows there will be setbacks, delays, frustrations, defeats, and errors. It is the Child that sits down to write a speech for the club or business group, can't immediately put his thoughts on paper, feels the agony of frustration, and gives up. The Child doesn't know the show business adage: "It takes twenty years to become an overnight success." The Adult knows that for every page that ends up in a good speech, there may be ten pages on the floor.

Can Admit to Being Wrong

The developed Adult ego state has the Critical Parent under control. It protects the Child from the fear of being wrong, the Child is under no threat, and so the person is able to say, "I was wrong." The healthy personality can stand back, take a look at himself, and have a good laugh at his own posturings, pratfalls, and pride. (In mental sickness, the person lacks this perspective. He often reasons in a tight little circle, he leaves out too much of reality; his sense of proportion is wrong.) The powerful Adult has awareness, he can observe himself objectively and self-correct. The powerful Adult knows the limitations of human knowledge, he knows that theories are just that—*theories*—which seem to explain how things are. People with a powerful Adult are often the wisest and the most tentative. Such people often have deep-seated humility; not that they go around declaring their humility, but you often find them actually *listening* to you. They seem to have an attitude that could be expressed in the words: "Maybe he's right."

The Adult Says, "I Intend to Live, Man, Do You Mind?"

A well-known comedian told in an interview about the days when he first began his career. He said many friends were scornful of his ambition and said he should forget becoming an entertainer, to which he always replied, "I'd like to try, man, do you mind?" He had a powerful Adult to protect his Child from ridicule. He refused to be restricted by the opinions of others.

Our Adult ego state can look at the world realistically and get tough with those who would limit us unnecessarily. It says, "I am me. I treasure what I am. I intend to expand my life. If, for some reason, you do not like me, then that is a problem *you* own. I intend to live, man, do you mind?"

Freedom Through the Adult Ego State

Remember, it is through our Adult ego state that we are able to free ourselves from the tyranny of the opinion of others and from our own inner tyranny. The genius of Eric Berne gave us Transactional Analysis, and one of his greatest discoveries was the Adult ego state. Frederick Perls gave us the "top dog" and "underdog," which could roughly be compared to the Parent and Child, but it was Berne who isolated the part of our personality that mediates between the other two and brings out the best in the total, integrated personality. The following are points to remember for the development of a powerful Adult ego state:

1. The Adult knows that problems are bound to happen and that life, for better or worse, is determined by the way these problems are handled. The Child is often surprised by problems and feels overwhelmed by them.

2. The Adult is solution-oriented, not problem-oriented. The Child may stand around feeling bad, wringing his hands. The Adult defines the problem as precisely as possible, gathers data, considers alternatives, looks for solutions.

3. The Adult is concerned with survival, but unlike the fearful Child, is able to experience a kinship with the rest of humanity. The Adult is committed to ethical and moral responsibility.

4. The Adult practices what I call the "there's more" philosophy. It knows that man's institutions and organizations are imperfect. It knows that much of man's knowledge has been built on mere theories that *seem* to explain how things are. It learns to live comfortably with uncertainty and is not alarmed by it. It knows

there is usually more on any subject than is at the disposal of human intelligence.

5. Knowing this, the Adult delays closure. It is able to entertain conflicting and opposite ideas at the same time. Ambiguity does not frighten it into making premature judgments.

6. The Adult knows about the Parent tapes. It knows that some of these tapes contain messages that may be out of touch with reality. The Adult examines the tapes to see which conform to reality, which are helpful, which are appropriate. The Adult turns the volume down on harsh or inappropriate tapes.

7. The Adult does not allow others to control the feelings of the inner Child.

8. As executive of the personality, the Adult ego state allows the person to respond appropriately from the OK parts of his Parent and Child, as well as from his Adult.

9. The Adult is aware of the inner dialogue and gives permission to ignore self-destructive messages. It offers options to the personality rather than:

Working himself to death.

Drinking himself to death.

Overeating.

Always losing (jobs, money, friends, in marriage).

Compulsive preoccupations (security, sex, money, status, aging, death).

10. The Adult gives the personality powerful permissions:

To enjoy.

To take time.

To experience setbacks without self-contempt.

To allow the creative and intuitive Child to operate.

To be "second dog" sometimes.

To be assertive when necessary.

To say "no" to unreasonable demands.

As you read through this book, you'll see many specific recommendations. Every chapter contains suggestions and ideas, either directly stated or presented in a real life story, which your Adult may wish to *remember* and *take action on* after you think about it more. There's a lively possibility your Parent or Child will sabotage this goal. Your Child may be fearful of change, or your Critical Parent may cut in and say, "Never mind that what he said about worrying seemed like it might work for you. He doesn't know your problems" or "How can you stop working yourself to death with your obligations?" or "Yeah, that's good marriage advice, but it's too late to help you."

To outsmart your Not OK Child and your Critical Parent, make a contract with yourself in your Adult for a specific change you are going to make in your life; then, when you're ready, move on to another specific contract in your Adult. Place a check beside those ideas you want to think about more after you have read the book through, or ideas you want to talk over with a friend, a loved one, your child or spouse. Make a note of the page number, and then come back and *do it.*

4

Your Self-Feelings

Your Child ego state is where your feelings reside.* Tell this to
an overworked executive, teacher, salesman, or housewife trying to
stay even in today's anxiety-ridden and competitive struggle, and
they might find it hard to believe that a knowledge of their Child
ego state can be of practical use. They would be wrong. You have
my assurance that if you learn to recognize, feel, control, and
protect the Child within you, it will be of more practical value in
your life than almost anything else you have ever learned.

Eric Berne said: ". . . the Child is . . . exhibited in two forms:
the *adapted* Child and the *natural* Child. The adapted Child is the
one who modifies his behavior under the Parental influence. He
behaves as father (or mother) wanted him to behave: compliantly
or precociously, for example. Or he adapts himself by withdrawing
or whining. Thus the Parental influence is a cause, and the adapted
Child an effect. The natural Child is a spontaneous expression:
rebellion or creativity, for example."†

In short, the adapted Child within you—and you have one,

---

*There are some exceptions to this that need not concern us at this point.
†Eric Berne, *Games People Play,* (New York: Grove Press, 1964) p. 26. In *What
Do You Say After You Say Hello?* (Bantam edition, p. 13), Berne shows the functional aspects of the Child ego state as: Natural, Adapted, and Rebellious. I concentrate on functional rather than structural analysis throughout this book.

whatever your age—is that part of you that learned certain behavior so you could survive and get along with the parental figures in your life. Maybe you learned to avoid people, or to try to please them all the time, or fight against them, or give in on everything. Your natural Child is that part of you that is a free spirit, spontaneous, creative, laughing, and fun-loving; it can also be selfish and aggressive.

But we're going to set aside further consideration of the natural and adapted Child for now. When I introduce the Child ego state to men and women, they quickly grasp what I have come to call their "self-feelings." You can recognize your inner Child if you think about it in terms of how you feel about yourself. You have three ways you feel about yourself, and they, to a great extent, determine your life. Your three self-feelings are:

OK Feelings.
OK If Feelings.
Not OK Feelings.

It is our self-feelings that determine how we feel about our life, ourselves and others, our career; they determine whether we have a warm or cold personality, how effective we are, what risks we take to expand our lives, how happy we will be.

The Self-Feeling Chart here is one of few charts in the book because, to me, many charts obscure what they are supposed to make simple. But this one doesn't, and I would like you to read it, identify some of your characteristics and goals in life, then determine whether they correspond with your self-feelings. Remember one thing: you can change your self-feelings. It's not as difficult as you might think, and I'm going to show you how.

The Not OK Self-Feelings

When you feel negative about yourself, you are in your Not OK Child ego state. There's considerable research showing that many

Self-Feeling Chart*

Self-feeling	Characteristics	Goals
OK Feelings	Open, aware, authentic	Truth
	Tolerant of mistakes	Growth
	Tentative, able to experiment	Helping others
	Spontaneous, autonomous	Greater awareness
	Relaxed, cooperative	I-Thou relationships
	Flexible, efficient	New challenges
	Fun-loving, enthusiastic	Expanded life
	Many interests	Enjoyment of life
	Lives in present moment	
OK If Feeling	Competitive, pressured	Power, prestige, status
	Threatened by achievements of others	Fame, adulation
	Fearful of mistakes	Others envy you
	Critical	Acceptance and approval
	Quantifies life: net worth, income, etc.	Conquests (in business, sex, politics, etc.)
	Worries, lives in future	Exploit others
	Must be "top dog," often overreaches	Get one-up
Not OK Feeling	Hostile	Put self down
	Envious	Put others down
	Self-conscious	Work against self
	Rigid	Hurt self
	Devious	Hurt others
	Defensive	Prove unworthiness of others
	Self-absorbed	Prove unworthiness of self
	Irritable	Be unhappy
	Suspicious	
	No self-disclosure	

*NOTE: While your self-feelings are in your Child ego state, some of the characteristics and goals are manifested in your Parent or Adult of us feel this way about ourselves. We go about feeling as if we are not quite up to all those others out there, that we can't win, that we are somehow one-down and all the rest are one-up. Not OK feelings are a weight around our neck, pulling us down, causing us to feel as if whatever headway we make must be as through a thick blanket of fog. Whenever we attempt something, we hold back a little for fear of failure; and we often stop short of success, just almost make it, because our anger (who wouldn't be angry if he's one-down with everybody?) is turned against those we must work with, or because we don't really think ourselves worthy of success. (How can you really be worthy if you aren't as good as others?)

The Not OK Child feels it is simply not good enough, often in a vague and ill-defined way. When the self-feelings are those of Not OKness, the personality tends to be either defiant, compliant, or sulking.* Some people spend most of their lives feeling Not OK. They don't know they are only a decision away from feeling OK.

People burdened with Not OK feelings were somehow treated shabbily as a child by the important people in their world. They were taught by thousands of words, gestures, facial expressions, innuendos, and punishments that they didn't measure up. In one form or another, they were given the message: "You are not what a person should be." As a result of these continuous messages, the child makes a decision, when he is much too young to make such decisions, that "they" out there are right: he really isn't up to standard.

The child grows up and forgets he made an unwise decision when he was very young to feel Not OK about himself. By now those feelings are a part of himself, they are just *him,* and if he ever wonders about himself at all, he probably brushes it off with:

*These three orientations of the Child correspond to the three basic personality maladjustments of Karen Horney's—i.e., moving against others, moving toward others, and moving away from others.

"That's the way I was born." The feeling diffuses his entire personality.

And so, carrying the weight of feeling negative about his very own being in a world where strokes are tightly rationed in the first place, the Not OK person struggles through life. An unfriendly glance, a mild disagreement, innocent joking, an insignificant gesture, a small failure, or a minor challenge, and he feels very bad and often lashes out. His wife, sweetheart, friends, children, or boss, often without knowing, invite* him to decide he will feel very bad about himself.

The person with Not OK self-feelings spends considerable time justifying his feelings about himself. He attempts little because he "knows" that Not OK people don't succeed, failures don't win, and so his life becomes a self-fulfilling prophecy; he attempts little, he therefore achieves little, and this proves to him that what he thought about himself was true.

People give feelings a holy power and are willing to remain a lifetime under their spell. Even if the person who feels Not OK experiences triumphs in his life, he tends to discount them, attributing them to luck or coincidence; you're not going to fool him that a Not OK person could accomplish what he did through ability; his feelings know better.

OK If Self-Feelings

Often people who are taught they are Not OK are invited to believe they have a conditional lease on life. They are told they can feel OK, at least temporarily, if they meet very strict conditions. They can feel OK as long as they meet unreasonable demands. The OK If conditions are impossible to fulfill on a continuing basis and violate psychological wisdom for healthy mental development.

Picture a neighborhood where many of the children are being

---

*Remember, if he owns his own feelings, no one can *make* him feel bad.

raised to believe they are OK If. In the house on the corner, the child is told he must do what his parents want him to do every minute of his life. His training is similar to that of a seal, except that when the required act is performed, the child gets a smile or nod of approval instead of a fish. In the house across the street the child is taught, verbally and nonverbally, that he is an unwanted nuisance and stands in the way of a carefree life for his parents, but he is OK *if* he does everything perfectly and makes no mistakes. Down the street, the parents let their little girl know she is OK *if* she does everything in half the time it should take. At the end of the block, the child keeps the giants reasonably calm if he shows no emotions. If he cries, shows affection, yells happily, or laughs loudly, they become upset. Across the way, the child is discovering his parents think he's OK *if* he is popular and well liked.

To the child, the messages are garbled, at first, but like a young animal seeking food, he doesn't take long to figure out what brings rewards and what brings disapproval, what brings smiles and what brings frowns. His ideas and behavior are shaped accordingly.

Gradually a transformation takes place. The child internalizes the messages that come from the important giants in his life. Their messages become his messages, and in time he forgets their origin. They become messages from the voice in his brain, and he plays them back to himself; the now grown child demands of himself unrealistic performance and achievement.

Such a person leads a conditional life. He allows himself to feel good about himself only if he meets the demands of the inner voice. It's a force driving him on with messages such as:

"You're OK *if* you don't make any mistakes."

"You're OK *if* you don't ever relax."

"You're OK *if* you're always top dog."

"You're OK *if* the right people approve of you."

"You're OK *if* you excel in everything."

"You're OK *if* everybody likes you."

"You're OK *if* you're always brave and never complain."

"You're OK *if* you never ask for anything."

"You're OK *if* you stay well"—sometimes it's if you stay sick.

Tension, Worry, and Conditional Living

Time is often a tyrant in the lives of OK If people. They have so much to do before they can feel good about themselves. The clock rides them from the moment they awaken until they sleep at night. Life is not something to be experienced and enjoyed, but something to be hurried through. They are often uneasy and impatient; they talk fast, interrupt others, don't listen when others talk to them.

OK If people often quantify their lives. After all, they have to keep track of how well they're doing. This means they live by numbers. They feel OK if they have a certain amount of money, if their house and car have the right price tags.

Those who lead conditional lives not only tyrannize themselves, but try to tyrannize those around them. If they think that perfection, hurry, blanket approval, etc., are the correct standards, then they demand these things not only of themselves, but of others as well. My guess is that the behavior of OK If people corresponds in some ways to that type of behavior categorized by Drs. Meyer Friedman and Ray Rosenman as "Type A" in their excellent book, *Type A Behavior and Your Heart.* I suspect that OK If people push up daisies earlier than the rest of the population.

There is a vast difference between the OK If feeling and normal ambition, between a driven person and one working to achieve a goal. The person in charge of his personality sets Adult goals that satisfy his total self; it's the difference between the politician driven by blind ambition to seek ever more power and glory, and the statesman dedicated to public service. The person in charge of his personality may, in his Adult, decide to work long hours to achieve his goal, but his Child will not feel the tension and strain because he does not feel he must succeed or be destroyed. This fear of destruction is understandable when you think, again, of the driven politician who, when he overreaches, as this type of person so often does, declares his life is over when he must leave office, even though he may only be leaving Washington to go back home to very comfortable living. What he means is that his Child feels crushed because it can no longer enjoy and search for ever greater power and glory. Other driven politicians commiserate with him, saying, "He has had everything taken from him," and to them, he has.

Kahler's "Drivers"*

Picture a basement, dark and dreary, where the negative feelings of suffering human beings are stored. The secret of a good life is to stay out of that basement and work and play in the sunshine. Taibi Kahler, Ph.D., a recognized TA theorist, says people can do this if they stay out of their "drivers," their conditional O.K. Dr. Kahler has identified five drivers which he says are the only doors that lead to that negative feeling basement. Once you get in any of the drivers, there's a good chance you'll end up down in the basement in one of your racket feelings: worry, guilt, depression, anger, inadequacy, confusion, hopelessness, etc.

How can you tell if you're under the influence of a driver?

Dr. Kahler says there are clues in facial expressions, words, tones, posture, and gestures. The five drivers that lead you down to your racket feeling are:

"Be perfect." A person under the influence of a "be perfect" driver is tense and seldom satisfied with his performance. No matter how well he is doing, he believes he should do better. He may keep meticulous records, adhere to inflexible schedules. His mouth is tight, his tone righteous, and his words clipped. He uses big words when small words would serve better. His posture is rigid, and his facial expression strained and stern. If he makes a mistake,

*Permission granted by Taibi Kahler, Ph.D., to include his "Drivers" concept as presented here.

he thinks he's not OK, rather than just calling it a mistake.

"Try hard." A person driven by "try hard" believes he can't get the job done. This driver has nothing to do with the fact that most of us must keep our nose to the grindstone. He struggles and tries hard instead of just *doing*. His stomach is tight, his shoulders tense; his tone is strained, and he may look perplexed and slightly distressed.

"Hurry up." A person under the "hurry up" driver is pressured by the sense of time passing. He believes he'll never get everything done that he should. His cry is that of the White Rabbit in "Alice in Wonderland," "Oh dear, oh dear I shall be too late. Oh my ears and whiskers, how late it's getting."

"Please me." Under the "please me" driver, the person feels he must get approval by pleasing others, even by pleasing everyone. All committees must be served on, everyone's needs must be met, and anticipated if possible. The person's own needs become secondary to him. He nods his head up and down vigorously so he can please the other person by showing how much he agrees, how well he understands, how willing he is to do the other's bidding.

"Be strong." A person under the influence of a "be strong" driver shows little emotion. His voice is monotone, his body rigid, and his face expressionless. He holds in his feelings and can't express any weakness. He can't tell someone he's hurt, upset, or tired.

When you are in a driver, you are, of course, leading a conditional life. You feel temporarily OK if you are perfect, try hard, hurry up, please others, or are always strong. When you live a conditional life, sooner or later you will fail. OK If people, people in their drivers, are living on parole, but they can't win because the terms of the parole demand the impossible; so it's certain to be revoked, with the person thrown into the prison of his Not OKness, sentenced once again to his small and familiar cell of hopelessness, depression, guilt, etc.

Feeling OK, or Release from Parole

A parolee can be released by a judge who grants him pardon. Your judge, the Critical Voice within, has no intention of doing that; so how do you set your Child free? Your Adult takes charge of your personality, sets the Child free, and then gives it powerful protection from the inner judge who will try to regain control. Your Adult says, in effect, "You are free. Go your own way."

Too simple? Well, let's go deeper. I said earlier a person's feeling of Not OKness resulted from a decision he made in his childhood when he was much too young to decide his worth as a human being. The Child decided he was Not OK, or OK only if he met unreasonable demands; he made this decision based on incomplete knowledge when he was barely able to function in his cognitive domain at all. Then he forgot he made this decision, and now all he has left is a pervading feeling of not being good enough. You may have made a decision you forgot you made. Your Adult can re-decide you are OK, period.

One Small Step to Freedom

Here's another way of looking at what we've just talked about. The idea is so important to our lives, I want to make sure we're together on this. As I said, when we're very small we make two basic decisions. One is about ourselves, and the other is about all those giants out there that inhabit the world of the small child; we decide whether or not we are OK and whether or not they are. And then we assume one of four life positions* based on what we decide:

---

*Eric Berne lists the positions in the following sequence: First Position: I'm OK, You're OK. Second Position: I'm OK, You're not-OK. Third Position: I'm not-OK, You're OK. Fourth Position: I'm not-OK, You're not-OK. Cf. Eric Berne, "Standard Nomenclature, Transactional Nomenclature," *Transactional Analysis Bulletin* vol. 8, no. 32 (October 1969), p. 112.

I'm Not OK—You're OK.

I'm Not OK—You're Not OK.

I'm OK—You're Not OK.

I'm OK—You're OK.†

I think you can see how the above decisions would be made by the very young mind depending on what was said to him and how those he depended on for his survival treated him. The child doesn't call his life position a decision, however; he just starts *feeling* that way about himself and others, and then does things that justify these feelings. Before he knows it, and unless he later examines these feelings, he may feel that way the *rest of his life*.

Now, if we could grow up feeling that we're OK and others are OK too, we would have it made.‡ Most of us either feel Not OK about ourselves, or we feel that others are Not OK, or both. And then the question arises: Do you really want to base the rest of your life, your feelings, thoughts, and behavior, on a life position taken by a very young child?

If you want to change, you can make a powerful decision. You decide your Child feelings are based on misinformation; they're out of date, archaic. You make a new decision in your Adult that I'm OK—You're OK. You decide this is your goal in life, your commitment, and that from now on this is the way you will view yourself and others. Don't let your Parent or Child override your Adult about this decision. You already know, in your Adult, it's the right one and it's buttressed by psychological theory, theology, philosophy, and common and current wisdom.

A word of warning: You will not always *feel* I'm OK—You're OK. It's like faith; you make a commitment, and when you have doubts, you remember your commitment. You remember you don't always *feel* what you have decided it is intelligent to feel.

†Cf. T. Harris, *I'm OK—You're OK;* Avon edition, p. 66.

‡Dr. Harris states that I'm Not OK—You're OK is the universal position of early childhood (op. cit., p. 67); however, there are TA theorists who disagree.

Don't worry about it. When you feel down on yourself, or down on others, decide to step over to your I'm OK—You're OK position. After you have done this a number of times, it becomes a habit.

You may be asking yourself what if you transgress your moral code—can you then say you're OK? I think you know the answer to that in your Adult. You and I know it isn't going to help if you stand around despairing the rest of your life. Condemn your behavior, but don't condemn yourself. When you transgress, start anew with your OK decision—make restitution, confess, atone, apologize, or whatever your standards call for, and remember you have decided you're OK. Do the same with others; in your mind, separate their behavior from their humanity.

Don't Climb Up—Step Over

It's important to realize that I'm OK—You're OK is a *decision* and not a *struggle.* Don't picture the OK position as the prize at the top of OK Hill. That would put us in the position of Sisyphus, the mythical king who was condemned to labor throughout eternity pushing a huge rock up a hill, only to have it fall back each time he neared the top.

Don't think of it like this:

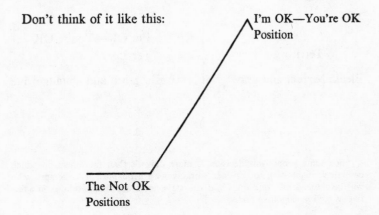

I'm OK—You're OK
Position

The Not OK
Positions

You see, if you picture getting OK as climbing a hill, then if you fight with your spouse, have trouble at work, are mean with your children, or get down on yourself for any reason, you feel: "Oh, no, I'm at the bottom of the hill again. Now I have to start over." You can understand why some people give up and decide to live at the bottom of the hill. It's too hard to do all that climbing.

If you picture getting OK as climbing, there's a chance you may have missed a crucial point. The Not OK positions are *feelings* based on incorrect decisions made in childhood. The I'm OK—You're OK position is a *decision* you make in your Adult. You don't, therefore, decide to try hard, struggle, or climb up to feeling I'm OK—You're OK; you simply decide that's your position. Then, when the Not OK feelings overwhelm you, you remind yourself of your I'm OK—You're OK decision and step back over the line. At first you may have to make that OK—OK decision over and over. You have to remember that you have made a decision about life, you now have a commitment.*

One side of the line is the Not OK territory and is bleak and barren. The other side is the OK side, lush and green with life in abundance. In your Adult, make the decision to live on the life-giving side.

Not OK Territory	I'm OK—You're OK Territory
Bleak, barren, and gray	Lush, green and abundant life

*For some people this decision is more difficult than for others, in which case they might wish to consider working with a qualified TA therapist who will help the Adult, *and the Child* ego state, in re-deciding, working on affective as well as cognitive areas.

Soaring

Once you practice making that small step over to the OK side, you'll experience a life that is as free, happy, and exhilarating as that of a soaring bird, or a glider pilot on a good day.

You see, you and I experience loneliness and emptiness in our lives because we have not been taught to love ourselves and others. But once we decide that we are OK and, in our Adult, monitor ourselves to see if we're living in the OK territory, then wonderful things happen in our lives. We don't have to fear showing our love, or giving kindness and attention, or making a speech, or accepting a challenge, or whatever, because we feel OK about ourselves. And we have a wonderful feeling inside of controlling our own lives because we know that if we should slip, if we fall on our faces, or someone rejects us, we do not have to start at the bottom of OK Hill. No, we are only a decision away from taking one small step back to the OK side. The more often we make that decision, the easier and more automatic it becomes.

Do you see how this can free you to soar above the clouds? Do you see how this frees you to be the very best *you* there is?

5

A Quick Way to
Improve Your Life

When you see a friend in the morning and say "Hello" to her, you have given her a small breath of life itself. You have recognized she exists. If you say, "Hello, Mary," you have given her more recognition; and if, in addition, you sit with her and listen with understanding to a problem she may have, or tell her she is important to you, you are giving her something that is psychologically therapeutic.

In TA all the activities connected with recognizing another person are called "strokes." When you give someone a positive stroke —a compliment, encouragement, attention, love, help—you give him a little more life; you give him courage. (The word "encourage" is of French derivation and could be translated literally "to give heart to.") Conversely, when you give someone a negative stroke, you invite him to feel bad. Either kind of stroke can be rejected, but because most of us are not as Sanforized as we should be, we usually accept negative strokes and allow ourselves to shrink a little.

The word "stroke" is sometimes used in a different sense than that used by TA practitioners. Some politicians and a few people in organizations have used it to mean an insincere compliment or reward for the purpose of manipulating. (People who treat others as things in an "I-It" relationship get momentary feelings of pleasure and power in controlling other people. They end up caught in their own trap, however, because they lose their own sense of humanity and regard themselves as an object as well.)

Stroke Deprivation

Most of us do not get enough strokes, and much of our time s spent trying to make up our stroke deficit. Unless we are badly bent, we want positive strokes; but lacking those, we will even settle for negative strokes rather than no strokes at all. One of the worst punishments for a human being is solitary confinement, out on the edge of the world alone, with no strokes received at all.

When human beings are stroke-deprived, they, in a psychological sense, shrivel up. They start perceiving their world in a negative, often hostile, way. This, of course, reflects in their human relations, which results in their getting even fewer strokes, and down they go, caught in a descending circle.

Stroking Is Life-Giving

Take, as an example, a man we'll call Don. As he wakes up early on a dark and cheerless morning, it flashes through his mind that because he is a mortal, his days are numbered. He isn't getting any younger, he's making no headway at work, and he's having difficulty getting along with his oldest teen-ager. It seems obvious that if Don could get a liberal dose of love and attention from his family right now, maybe no more than a minute's worth, things might look up for him. If he had a heart attack or was seriously injured, his family would rally round him; but we have little experience recognizing and treating psychological injuries in our families. What Don needs is positive stroking, but the chances are he will set himself up for negative strokes during the day. Often when we most need love, attention, and kindness, we are the most unlovable. If Don could communicate with his wife on a meaningful level, he could tell her he has a stroke deficit. He could say something to the effect: "Honey, I feel middle-aged today. It looks like one of the younger guys is getting ahead of me at the office. I not only look old, I feel old. How about a stroke?"

In a class or workshop when I talk about one person asking another for a stroke, whether it's a group of teachers, business men and women, or whoever, it always gets a laugh. It strikes people as humorous, in our culture, to ask for recognition and love. We're so accustomed to hiding our needs that the thought of openly admitting them makes us uncomfortable and embarrassed.

Don't underestimate the importance of stroking for yourself, your friends, and your loved ones. It's not an exaggeration to say that strokes can be life-giving. Infants sometimes develop a condition called marasmus when they are deprived of physical attention. They need touching, handling, and fondling by other human beings for their survival. As adults our stroking needs are more complex and varied than that of infants, but we still need to be told we're OK through recognition, attention, understanding, and reassurance. Lack of stroking plays a major role in depression. People suffering from depression sometimes improve remarkably when they are given special attention and love.

Stroking in Organizations

The famous Hawthorne experiments demonstrated years ago that people in organizations want attention and recognition for their work. Business school students across the country, and also many psychology students, learn the details of these long and involved experiments which started in 1928 when Elton Mayo of Harvard went to the Hawthorne plant of the Western Electric Company in Cicero, Illinois. I won't go into all the findings, but the Illumination experiment will give you the gist of what is known as the Hawthorne Effect. Mayo and his assistants wanted to determine the effect of lighting on the workers' production, and conducted tests at different levels of illumination to see which level produced the optimum amount of work. To their surprise, production kept going up no matter what the level of lighting. Even at the level of one candlepower, production kept climbing. The lighting wasn't important to the workers; it was the fact that someone was interested in what they were doing. It was the attention they received.

Whatever the level of organization we work on, we have essentially the same human needs. If you want to know what the lowest or the highest worker wants, merely look within yourself to your own needs. We all want attention, recognition, appreciation, and praise.

Stroking Patterns

We all need strokes, but we differ in the amount we require and in the way we give and receive them. Some of us were stroke-deprived in our childhood and are so insecure that we need almost constant stroking to feel comfortable. Like puppies, a pat on the head fills us with joy, and an angry glance sends our spirit slinking to the basement. One woman told me she feels rebuffed when her cat gets up and walks away from her.

But it isn't humorous really. A woman craving daily strokes, married to Mr. Silent Inscrutable, who gives her a compliment every fourth year, suffers greatly. She feels desperately alone and unwanted. And a man or woman, after a day spent working at Parched Routines, Incorporated, or a child home from Prickly Elementary School, craves to know he is human again and treasured as an individual.

Some Can't Receive Strokes

A person with a strong Not OK feeling has difficulty accepting positive strokes. Since he has convinced himself he's Not OK, he wonders what your angle is in giving him a stroke, telling him he's OK. Like Sherlock Holmes examining evidence, he whips out his magnifying glass and looks over the stroke you gave him. It doesn't fit into his perception of himself, and so he rejects it. He will be quick to accept a negative stroke, though, even reaching out to grab one where none was intended. It's very hard to get a positive stroke through to a person who feels Not OK, but he'll remember a negative stroke for years.

Some people have to evaluate strokes to decide whether they are worth accepting. They only count big strokes from big folks. A child waving hello to them doesn't register. They're looking for a nod from the president of the yacht club, or a person higher up the ladder.

Some Can't Give Strokes

Some people never learned as children about giving love, attention, understanding, or praise to others. In their family it wasn't the thing to do. You kept your mouth shut and your feelings to yourself. It doesn't often occur to them to give someone a stroke, but even when they do think of it, they feel too self-conscious to go ahead and let one slip away. Others don't like to give strokes because they're afraid of being rejected. Just think how humiliating it would be if you gave away a smile and a "hello" without having it returned. A person who feels Not OK would accept this as a discount and might choose to feel bad about it.

Then there are others, who are reluctant to give strokes because somewhere they got the mistaken idea that a thorough investigation should precede each stroke to make certain it is correct, accurate, and deserved. They don't have time for that much research, and besides, it might work against them. Tell somebody they're doing a good job, and the first thing you know, they might ask for a raise, or stop trying to please. How little they know about motivation! Most people are willing to work harder when they know their efforts are appreciated. Where there is an absence of praise, people usually feel: "To hell with you; I'm sick of trying to please you."

Finally, there are those who don't give strokes to others because they are not *there* with the other person. They are in a hurry, living in future time, and don't really see and hear other people. People are nothing more than objects or means to an end to such individuals.

Some Give Negative Strokes

The stroke miser is bad, but the negative stroker is worse. Like a flamethrower, he scorches everything in his path. "See you're putting on quite a bit of weight, aren't you, George?" "Why do you suppose Mary dislikes you so much?" "You never were much of a cook, Gladys." "Sally is the image of her father, with that large nose and receding chin." "I'm glad to do things for you even though you never thank me." Sometimes you can't believe you heard right as you slink off down the street. After you get home you think of brilliant ripostes you could have made. People who give negative strokes are usually feeling Not OK about themselves. They think they'll feel less Not OK if they can make you feel Not OK too. Some try to make a virtue out of their "candor." They disguise their hostility with the romantic notion: "I'm the kind of person who doesn't mind letting people know what I think."

How to Be Lonely

The demand for a negative stroker is slight. Life is demanding enough without such a person around, whether he is parent, spouse, in-law, acquaintance, or whoever. A man or woman who practices handing out negative strokes, diminishing his fellow man, runs the danger of shrinking himself as well, so that after a time there will be no part of him left to turn off his incessant meanness, nothing that can end his hellish isolation.

Your Defense Against Negative Strokes

You can defend yourself against negative strokes by *choosing* not to be hurt by them. You become very powerful once you are able to take this important step in your life. Your Adult, in effect, intercepts the negative stroke before it penetrates to hurt your Child, and decides what to do with it. If the negative stroke has some informational value that you can use to improve your life, you may choose to accept it; otherwise, you discard it and refuse to take it seriously. And you never hand the negative stroke over to your internal Critical Parent to be used against you: "See, I told you you aren't good enough, and now it's been confirmed."

It's important to assume responsibility for your feelings. You don't pass out keys to your front door, and you shouldn't pass out keys to your feelings so that anyone can barge in at any time and ruin your day. You belong to yourself, so why give remote control of your feelings to others? Why let someone else decide how you will feel? We give others too much power over us when we say, "You made me angry," "You hurt my feelings," "I was in a good mood until you came along," etc. We experience freedom when we change that to: "I have decided not to allow you to hurt my feelings."

You Can Decline the Invitation

It's inevitable that some people are going to invite you to feel bad. You might say, "My wife [husband, child, mother, father] *made* me feel bad." But stop a minute before you say this and think how insignificant, powerless, and small that makes you. Do you see how, as your Adult becomes powerful, you can view all negative strokes as mere *invitations* to feel bad, invitations which you are powerful enough to decline?

One of my favorite stories about refusing an invitation is about the author William Faulkner. When he was asked to dinner at the White House, he declined, saying, "I'm too old at my age to travel that far to eat with strangers."* This, to me, is a humorous example of a person declining a powerful invitation. The next time you're invited to feel a certain way that is not life-giving, put your Adult in charge and refuse the invitation. You might find it helpful to remember Faulkner's refusal of the White House invitation.

How to Enrich Your Life

1. Give strokes freely. The supply is unlimited. The more you give, the more you get, and the more you have. Recognize the good in others and tell them about it.

2. Listen to others. Really listen, enter their world and perceive as they perceive. Listening is one of the highest forms of stroking.

3. Talk about stroking within your family. Tell them your needs and ask about theirs. Stroking needs are rooted deep in psychological theory. Be clinical; refuse to be embarassed about open discussion of them.

4. Learn to accept good strokes. Take them at face value, internalize them, remember them. It's really a downer to the person who gave you a stroke if you reject it. You're telling him the stroke he offered is worthless to you.

5. Give yourself strokes. Treasure your *self.* Congratulate yourself on a job well done; you don't have to wait for a great accomplishment. My grandmother never made a meal she didn't compliment herself on, and my wife always laughs at her own jokes. This is part of enjoying your *self.*

*Joseph Blotner, *Faulkner: A Biography* (New York: Random House, 1974), p. 1821.

6. Don't collect negative strokes. Look them over. If they aren't helpful to you, throw them out. The decision is *yours.*

7. Don't pass out negative strokes. When you give a negative stroke, you'll usually get it back in spades. Just remember you're OK, and others are too.

Relationships improve when stroking patterns improve. If you learn to give authentic, positive strokes and learn to take them in, you can enrich your life and the lives of those around you.

Dr. Hedges Capers and his wife, Betty, of La Jolla, California, are an inspiring team who travel around the world holding TA workshops. I attended one of their three-day workshops in 1974 and afterwards talked about strokes with Dr. Capers. It is his firm belief that an autonomous person can take in those strokes he wants and reject all the discounts and negative strokes that subtract from his life and happiness. Dr. Capers is convinced that when you get above the level of strokes you need to feel OK, you can even put them in the "bank."

Remember this, if you ignore the importance of stroking, you will do damage to the people who matter to you, and to yourself. A vital part of you will shrivel up and die.

Self-Stroking

You can start now being nicer to yourself. Don't tell yourself you don't have time. If you don't take care of your inner Child, it will trip you up somehow. This is true whether you're a housewife, a single man or woman, or president of one of *Fortune*'s top 500 companies. In an article by Michael Maccoby in *Fortune*'s December 1976 issue, the subheading states that "as managers rise through the hierarchy . . . they develop their intellects but not their emotions. Careerism produces flabby-hearted executives, empty lives, and hazards for society." The article, titled "The Corporate Climber Has to Find His Heart," goes on to say that "he eventually loses touch with his deepest strivings." Many corporations, large and small, have trained professionals conducting TA seminars and workshops to help their executives and other employees use the full range of their personalities.

An overdeveloped Adult that excludes the Child is not even practical. It can result in such distressing symptoms as sleeplessness, overeating, anxiety, depression. No matter how tough-minded a person may imagine himself to be, he cannot ignore his Child and get away with it. To start with, do some things that please you for the fun of it. Make a list of what makes you happy and do them. Go fishing, buy a model train, start an antique collection, try a new hair style, take piano lessons, go to the beach, paint a picture, buy a bird feeder, visit Disney World, buy a *Mad* magazine, take a trip. Remember, your Child is ageless. Take good care of your Child in these and other ways and you'll not only enjoy life; you'll probably live longer and be more effective.

6

How to be a Winner at Work

It is estimated that every single year as many as 250,000 executives are fired.* For the most part, they are not fired because they are incompetent. Nor are they fired because they lack knowledge in their field or are undereducated. After spending several years and thousands of dollars studying why men and women are passed over for promotion or fired, a major Eastern university concluded that in most cases it was because they couldn't get along with other people.

The following is a true story about a top executive who was fired. We'll call him Mike because that isn't his name, but everything else about the story is essentially true. Mike is one of the 250,000 executives who lose their jobs each year through either a forced resignation or an actual firing. (In *The Executive Life,* the Editors of *Fortune* state: "The vast majority of resignations—perhaps four out of five—are forced; that is, they are in fact firings.")†

Mike has now been out of work a year. Statistically, he's one of the 250,000, but when you look closely at him and his family and

*Alan N. Schoonmaker, *Anxiety and the Executive* (American Management Association, © 1969, p. 118.

†The editors of *Fortune,* *The Executive Life* (Garden City, New York: Doubleday, 1956), p. 187.

what Mike's firing has done to them—Mike losing his drive and self-esteem, bickering in the household, his wife back at a job she doesn't like, a daughter dropping out of college, a son not finishing graduate school—he becomes much more than a statistic. The quarter-million men and women and their families are a recurring national tragedy and an indictment of our educational system, which often ignores the needs of the people it is supposed to serve.

These firings occur because men and women have been given little instruction in how to get along with other people. They are not taught how to understand themselves and others. The few courses they have in human relations are incomplete. They are given course after course in computer science and operations research, but very little about understanding and working with human beings.

Mike holds a master's degree in Business Administration and, as he said later, not one professor had ever given him meaningful instruction in understanding himself and those he worked with. To use Mike's words: "In many ways my graduate education was useless—a farce—covering subject matter I have never used, taught by people who had no idea how business really worked."

A knowledge of TA would not save all the 250,000 executives fired each year or the countless thousands of additional people fired in supervisory and middle management positions. But in my opinion, it would save a large percentage of them. Here is Mike's story.

Why Mike Was Fired

Mike was forty-three, and lived in Miami with his wife and four children. In addition to their house in Miami, they owned a beautiful cottage in Punta Gorda, on the west coast of Florida. As president of a small bank, Mike could regulate his own hours so that he and his family could take off late Thursday or early Friday morning for a long weekend of swimming and fishing.

Mike, in short, had it made.

Mike's predecessor had died suddenly of a heart attack, and the board of directors had chosen Mike as his replacement. They selected him; they were not rubber-stamp management-slate directors. In the five years Mike was president, the assets of the bank doubled—not a bad record for Mike, but not as outstanding as it might appear, because many other banks had done as well in the booming Florida economy.

Mike thought he was underpaid, and he wanted a pension plan. The directors delayed on both counts. Their reason is unknown, but they evidently thought Mike was hurrying things along a little too fast.

Mike discussed the situation with his wife, but on this subject they were both on tapes. Their Adult ego state was inoperative here. They passed remarks back and forth such as:

"I'm the one who built that bank."

"They would have a devil of a time replacing me."

"Who do they think they are?"

"We're making peasant wages compared to some presidents of banks this size."

Mike spent considerable time in his Child ego state concerning his raise and the pension plan. He felt hurt that they wouldn't give him more. He felt they didn't recognize the good job he was doing. It made him angry that they would withhold something he thought he should have. Had he been aware of it, he would have seen that his feelings were much the same as a small child's when he can't have a second piece of cake.

One day during a directors' meeting, Mike's Parent ego state took over, and he said something to the effect that he considered it a "must" that he get both his raise and a pension plan. It was said during a time when money was extremely tight. The economy had slowed down, and the directors were edgy about a few large loans they had made.

The chairman of the board asked Mike, "What do you mean by 'must'?"

Mike's Parent replied, "Just that."

Mike was asked to leave the room and when he returned the directors asked for his resignation. Here, Mike's Child obliged. "If that's the way you want it, it's OK with me," replied the hurt little boy within Mike.

And with those few maneuverings by his Parent and Child ego states, Mike blew his whole deal. Mike was acting like a child, insisting on a pay raise and pension, but it goes deeper than that. He was hypnotized. Mike was under a spell and couldn't see reality.

When Mike was small, his mother hammered into him, "You mustn't ever let anyone take advantage of you." Mike's mother had a hard life, and she was bitter. She felt everyone took advantage of her and her husband. Mike's father showed him how to carry out the warning of his mother. He taught Mike to haggle over every price. By example, he showed Mike that unless you were angry over the wages you were receiving, you were not a man.

Mike had these ideas recorded in his brain as surely as if he had had an operation implanting them there. Years later, these voices played in his head, telling him: "Those directors are taking advantage of you." "Don't let them get away with that." "You're not much of a man if you don't demand the money due you."

Now that the voices have subsided, and he is no longer employed by the bank, Mike can observe the situation from his Adult. Looking back, he thinks he must have been out of his mind to give up such a sweetheart of a deal. He can't imagine why he did what he did.

Mike was out of his mind to the extent that he was out of touch with reality. His Adult was disconnected on this point. It happens when we're driven by old Parent tapes or archaic feelings left over from childhood, instead of putting the Adult ego state in charge as executive of the personality.

How Foster Saved His Job

Foster was luckier than Mike. He is in middle management with one of *Fortune*'s top 500 companies (in fact, one of the top 100). His yearly salary provides a comfortable living. One night after class when a few of the students had come over to my house, Foster opened the conversation by saying, "TA saved my job." The other students were interested in his story, and naturally I was pleased that something I had taught had such practical and immediate application to Foster's life; so we asked him to tell us the story in detail.

"My trouble started a long time ago," said Foster. "I was kicked around as a child by a sometimes drunken mother and an abusive father. As a result, I've got a lot of hostility in me. But I've been aggressive as hell and partly because of this have had a certain amount of success. [Foster is also very bright.]

"The hostility has caused me trouble from time to time. I lose my temper easily, and as a result, over the years I've told off a few bosses and stormed off jobs. Luckily, I was able to land other good jobs, and my career didn't suffer too much.

"Well, it almost happened again last Friday. I've been having trouble with the person I report to. He's been getting under my skin. I felt he was pushing me around.

"It came to a head on the phone Friday when he cut me off and said he didn't have time to discuss a problem I brought up. My temper flashed, and I hung up on him and told my secretary I would be damned if I would take that kind of crap.

"Then for the first time in my life I actually *felt* what I was doing. I *listened in* to myself and knew what had happened. I had been letting the Critical Parent of others hook the Not OK Child within me all my life, and then, as I had finally done with my father when I was old enough, telling them to go to hell. All the pain was self-caused. As I listened to myself I knew all I had to do was say, 'I'm OK and what you say won't bother me.' When I knew this I asked myself, in my Adult ego state, what a reasoning person might do in this case. The answer was obvious. I picked up the phone, called my boss and apologized. Sure enough, when I approached him in my Adult, he came back Adult and said that he had been the one in error.

"I've made up my mind," continued Foster, "that as soon as I finish this class, I'm going to join a TA workshop. I'm sure it will make me more effective."

As a footnote to this story, Foster did join a TA workshop when he finished my class. I gave him the names of two excellent TA therapists, one a man and the other a woman, who have been trained and certified by the International Transactional Analysis Association.

He has called me several times since that class. He has had two promotions and is now one step from top management. The last time he called he told me, "I'm dead certain that your teaching me the application of TA to business kept me from blowing my job as I had several times in the past. It gives me a tool to handle my anger and hostility. In addition, the TA therapist helped me to feel the forces within me at work. It went beyond the intellectual level. I'm certain TA has been one of the reasons for my recent promotions."

Why Ben Was Passed Over

Being passed over can be as serious a blow to a man or woman as being fired. Here again, we are talking about rejection. This is Ben's problem, and he feels desperate about it. All his life he has struggled to be successful in his work. Twenty years ago, right out of college, he joined the company he now works for. He has worked hard all this time, likes his job, gets along well with people, and has gradually risen to a position of importance in his organization. An outsider looking at Ben's life would call him a success.

But Ben doesn't feel that way; or rather, Ben's inner Child doesn't feel that way. Over the past few years he has gradually become more and more discontented with his lot in life. Ben is too confused to know when his dissatisfaction started. If he could operate in his Adult on the matter, he would see that it could be traced back to the time, several years ago, when the president of his company retired and the board of directors started looking around for a replacement.

Ben was one of the senior vice presidents and, along with two other men, was in the running for the top job. But Ben was passed over. The job was given to a vice president who had been with the company less than half the time Ben had. He was also younger than Ben.

Ben thought he had adjusted to missing out on the presidency. His Adult rationalized that the board obviously wanted a younger man and someone with more sales experience. The new president and Ben got along fine, so there was no threat to Ben's position within the company, and in addition, Ben was given a handsome raise. About the only thing Ben had to face up to was the fact that he would probably never be top man at his company.

But from the time Ben was passed over, his life became dull and tasteless. For Ben the zest is gone; his life seems to have lost its meaning. The difficulty is not with Ben's intelligence; he's a smart man. He has known all along the odds against becoming president. Even recently he gave it considerable thought when he read an article in *Fortune* magazine on the narrowing opportunities at the top of the corporate pyramid. But Ben's inner Child was always waiting for the next promotion. If Ben didn't get a promotion every few years, then Ben's Parent would beat down on his Child and tell him he wasn't worthwhile.

As long as life was an unbroken series of steps up, Ben's Critical Parent could be kept mollified. Ben's OK If message from his Parent tapes was: "You're entitled to feel you're an OK person *if* you keep climbing higher and higher." Now the messages inside Ben's head tell him he has failed. The Parent says: "I told you you didn't have it in you to go all the way to the top." And the Not OK Child answers: "Yeah, you're right. I'm not much of a person. If only I had handled things better."

The inner Child experiences contempt when it doesn't meet the unreasonable demands of the inner Critical Parent. This inner voice, since it is a recorded message, ignores the circumstances that cause us to fall short and places no value on accomplishments already achieved, no matter how considerable they may be. With his Adult in charge, Ben needs to nurture himself, distinguish between a disappointment and a catastrophe, and prevent his Child from flooding him with feelings inappropriate to the situation.

Rules to Follow if You Suffer a Setback

Foster kept his job and received several promotions, Mike lost his job, Ben was passed over. For those who are unlucky as Mike and Ben were, TA can be of help. Being fired from a job is one of the most painful events to befall a man or woman; it's a devastating rejection. Looking for another job is often humiliating, and so is missing a promotion.

You can, however, when you suffer a setback, cut your losses short. You can make certain that a job, a promotion, an opportunity, is all you lose, and not your self-respect as well. You can make it as painless as possible, by following these rules:

1. Realize that during a setback your Critical Parent may pounce. With full force it will berate your Not OK Child and cause you to feel self-contempt and despair. Turn off these Critical Parent tapes or you'll find that just when you need to be "up," you'll be immobilized by self-hatred.

2. The Critical Parent messages will include: "They finally found out about you." "You really messed up." "Nobody will want you now." "You should have worked harder." "You can't even support your family." "No one will give you a recommendation." These must be turned off, ignored, and counteracted.

3. Renew often your decision "I'm OK." Your Child feelings may tell you otherwise. Don't listen. (See "One Small Step to Freedom" in Chapter 4.)

4. Keep in mind the expectations of the Child. When it's fearful, it paints a black and hopeless picture. Your Child feelings will tell you, "You'll never be happy again."

5. Your fearful Child may panic and make irrational decisions. Right after a setback don't make important moves, such as quitting your job, moving to another area, etc., unless you have to.

6. Make certain your Adult computes accurately. Avoid generalities such as: "There are no opportunities with this organization." "There just aren't any jobs now." "No one wants an older executive." "They only want young secretaries."

7. Do everything possible to reinforce your OK decision about yourself. Keep to a routine. Don't cut expenses (unless absolutely necessary) that help you feel OK. Have lunch, take cabs, go out to dinner. Give your hurt Child time to recover.

8. Give and receive stroking. If you allow your Parent tapes to turn on you, they will turn on others. Don't allow this to happen. Give your family extra strokes, and they'll give you extra strokes in return.

Losers Are Disappointed and Play "Ain't It Awful"

There are many differences between winners and losers in organizations, but several stand out. Losers have Child expectations inappropriate to life on this planet and because of this they drown themselves in disappointment. They move from organization to organization, trying to find the ideal situation where everyone is reasonable, kind, and sincere, and where justice reigns.

Losers wait around for the perfect situation to come along, while winners expect conditions in organizations to be, at best, half sane and work from there. Losers are *shocked* when the boss turns out to be a drunk, or the company is sold, or the government institutes an unreasonable rule, or they receive an unexpected and critical memo. The slightest disturbance causes the loser to disconnect his Adult while he plays "Ain't It Awful." Once again, his Child has been surprised and hurt by the lack of perfection in his fellow man, and because of his disappointment, he has no interest in anything save marveling over, and suffering a little because of, the defects of mankind:

> Ain't it awful about the boss.
> Ain't it awful the way they run things around here.
> Ain't it awful how dumb they are.
> Ain't it awful they don't recognize my work.
> Ain't it awful I'm not promoted.
> Ain't it awful the way they waste money.
> Ain't it awful the way I'm treated.
> Ain't it awful I was criticized.

Losers, because their Child is angry or resentful that once again their expectations have not been met, keep their Adult inoperative and repeat the problem over and over. Winners shrug their shoulders and start figuring what they can do under the new set of circumstances.

How to Increase the Odds on Winning

If you practice the following, it won't ensure that you'll be a winner in your organization, but I guarantee it will increase your chances of winning.

1. Lower your expectations of others. Many people you work with are handicapped emotionally (they feel Not OK about themselves) and because of this their actions surprise and puzzle you. If you can, help them; but if you can't help them, don't let them deter you from reaching your goal by triggering your Not OK feelings.

2. Remember that losers repeat the problem over and over; winners look for solutions. Winner training consists of breaking this habit so that you automatically will think: "I'm sure I can handle this. Let's see, what should I do next? Do I have alterna-

tives?" (More about this in Chapter 8: A New Way to Solve Problems.)

3. Remember that when you play "Ain't It Awful" you are on tapes. The organization you work for is bound to be less than perfect for the simple reason that it is staffed with people. Don't waste time bemoaning the times you live in; they are the only times you'll ever have.

4. Train yourself to expect the unexpected. Delays, upsets, misunderstandings, criticism, injustice, and slights happen to human beings. The loser is surprised and allows his Child feelings to be triggered by each event. The winner does not give others remote-control buttons on his feelings.

5. Remember that winners have a plan, which includes knowing what to do if they lose. Winners know what to do *next*. Losers are overwhelmed by adverse circumstances. Their fearful or resentful Child feelings take over their personality and they have no idea at all how to handle their bad luck.

6. Remember that winners *think*. Steve Seplocha, city editor of my home-town newspaper, is one of the most effective "natural" managers I've ever met. He sees many winners and losers in the course of a year. He has over fifty reporters he assigns stories to, and he says you can quickly separate those who will eventually become great reporters from the ones who will remain mediocre. "Give a good reporter an assignment," says Steve, "and his attitude is that he can handle it. If you tell the mediocre ones to check an out-of-town story, by the time you're through answering their questions about where to find out-of-town directories, how to spell 'Xenia,' who to charge the call to, you wish you had handled the story yourself." Steve believes, as do many effective managers, that if you tell winners the "what," they will figure out the "how" themselves.

7

One More Time, How Do You Communicate?

The Boss Who Learned to Communicate

During a period of several days, while working with an organization on improving communication, I met an executive I'll call Sam. Sam represents thousands of men and women who are bright, able to think under stress, make complicated plans, organize their work, and weigh risk/reward ratios. However, many of these people, whatever level they are on in the place they work, have one major problem. They simply don't know how to communicate with the people they work with. For that matter, they don't know how to communicate with their friends or loved ones.

Sam—and those like him—could not communicate for the same reason that he can't fix the engine of his car. It has nothing to do with intelligence. He simply doesn't have words and concepts at his disposal concerning car engines, nor did he have any training in communication.

Sam, the same as the rest of us, has often heard that many of the problems in business, marriage, child-raising, whatever, are caused by poor communication, but no one had ever told Sam specifically how to communicate. He always assumed that good communication meant that you tell someone what you want them to do and that's all there is to it. Sam, in other words, assumed things about human behavior that simply are not true.

There's a well-known Harvard Business School case in which a Mr. Post is hired as the vice president of purchasing for the Dashman Company and immediately sends a letter to the purchasing executives in each of the twenty plants of the company telling them to notify him of all purchasing contracts in excess of ten thousand dollars at least one week in advance of the date on which they are to be signed.

During the two weeks that follow the sending of the letter, Mr. Post hears from all but a few plants that they will cooperate. Sounds like communication has taken place, doesn't it? Mr. Post sends a specific, well-written order to the twenty plants and is assured they will comply.

Unfortunately, during the next six weeks Mr. Post receives not one notice from any plant that contracts are being negotiated and, presumably, sits alone and brooding in his inactive office while the plants continue operating exactly as they did before his letter. Mr. Post is not a real executive; he just plays a role. He acts as he thinks a V.P. should act—crisp, decisive, issuing detailed orders—and his act could cost him his job.

Communication does not automatically take place when one person gives detailed instructions and the other acknowledges he understands the instructions. Good communication does not start with talking, nor with sending letters and memos. *Good* communication starts with listening—what I call Creative Listening, finding out what the other person thinks and feels and how he may behave. When Sam wishes to *communicate* with someone, he must enter that person's world, look at things as he does, and feel what that person is feeling. Or, in the Dashman case, Mr. Post must enter the world of the plant managers and their purchasing executives.

Perhaps your Critical Parent voice is saying, "How can I enter someone's world when I'm in a hurry and only want a simple task performed?" The answer, of course, is that when you're in a hurry and you want someone to do something simple, you don't really need to communicate; you merely tell him what you want him to do. But I'm talking about a higher level of communication, about things that are very important, and I'm also talking about a person who decides that on some things he wants to be a leader; he wants to inspire, and not just exercise his authority. I think some of the best communication takes place where you inspire people and motivate them.

Suppose, in business, you want a salesman or woman to sell more; *you* have a desire that someone else sell more. In other words, *you* are motivated. So you call the salesperson in and say, "Harry, you have to make more calls. You have to sell more. You simply have to get with it." Do you really think that transfers the motivation slug from inside you to inside Harry, where it needs to be? Of course it doesn't. It may scare Harry into thinking you may fire him. It may cause him to lose his confidence in himself, it may cause him to quit; but whatever it causes, you have not found out why Harry isn't selling more. You have not found out the nature of Harry's problem. Harry is a salesman, so he already knows he is supposed to sell. If you can enter his world, you may discover what the obstacle is, and *then* you can motivate him.

Executives who wish to communicate, who wish to motivate, must remember that when they give an order, this means *they* are already motivated; they have a desire. The trick for executives who wish to increase their effectiveness and become professional managers of human behavior is to get the motivation inside the other person. Fortunately, we now—for the first time, really—have a specific tool in TA that intelligent people can immediately put to use for communicating and motivating.

Whenever I work with organizations, I accept short-term contracts with the stipulation that I will not only hold group meetings, but also have the privilege of working with the men and women individually if they are willing and if I think a short private session might be helpful. TA is so powerful, and its application so easily understood, that sometimes a twenty-minute conversation over a cup of coffee, with a few specific exercises recommended, plus several pass-out sheets, give people new insights into their lives. So many people seem to feel that they must work with a feeling of stress; they deny their feelings, they overcontrol themselves and others, they become hardened in self-destructive behavior that they think, mistakenly, helps them reach their goal.

Sam, the executive I was talking about, and I spent several hours one afternoon talking, and I showed him the new TA way to communicate. It is by far more effective than anything I have seen in the fields of communication, advanced management theory, or industrial psychology. I drew several diagrams especially for him. Sam learned TA as quickly as he learned most things in his life, and I could tell it was not just intellectually, so that he could toss off a few phrases as people do who wish to parade their knowledge, such as: "Oh, sure, I know about Carl Rogers. He's client-centered therapy" or "Yeah, Maslow is self-actualization" or brush Skinner off with "reward and punishment." No, Sam learned TA not only intellectually, but affectively; he could actually feel what he was feeling.

Sam can now turn conversations that are going wrong into Adult-to-Adult communication. He learned how to protect his Not OK Child and how to keep from hooking the Not OK Child in others. He learned how to—hold on, now—nurture himself and those who work for him (executives who do this are very practical people), and he learned how to set an atmosphere, with his Critical Parent turned off, where those he works with, and also his wife and children, can open up and tell what is on their minds. He no longer enters his house as the executive Critical Parent, full of orders and demands for routine and perfection. He understands why this can't possibly work in a household and prefers the "trade-off," as he aptly calls it, of giving up a few meaningless Critical Parent tapes and receiving love and understanding in return.

Perhaps most important to Sam is that he has learned he can reach his goals faster by taking care of the Child, the most valuable part of the personality, that exists within himself and within the men and women he works with, as well as the Child within the members of his family. He communicates not only with others now, but with himself as well. He still doesn't know how to fix his car, but he now has a vocabulary and a technique for understanding himself and fixing faulty human relations.

Rules for Creative Listening:

1. Creative Listening is nonevaluative and noncritical. Your goal is understanding the other person, not judging him.

2. The climate you set must be nonthreatening. (No one tells the truth to a hanging judge.) Parents, for example, who severely punish their children and then wonder why they are lied to have little understanding of the human animal. Lying is often a child's only possible defense to escape oppressive punishment.

3. Keep the line of communication open by emphasizing "you" and not "I." For example:

"How do *you* feel about that?"
"How does the situation seem to *you?*"
"How did *you* feel then?"
"What do *you* think you should do?"

4. Ask for confirmation to check whether you're hearing correctly, with:

"It seems bad to you, right?"
"Am I right in saying you feel this way?"
"Is this the way you see the problem?"

The rigid personality feels threatened easily and does not practice Creative Listening. His relationships at home will be strict and authoritarian rather than loving and undestanding. At the office he may exercise the authority given him by the organization, but he will not be a leader. Perhaps the saddest thing to befall such a person is loneliness; he never knows who anyone really is or what they really think and feel.

Your Memos Give You Away

If an executive sends too many memos, if every day there is a blizzard of written directives from his office, it could mean:

1. His Critical Parent drives him to get everything neat, in order, perfectly understood. This tape will cause him to have neat files full of carefully spelled out rules and regulations. It will also cause him to be so out of touch with reality that sooner or later he may hurt the organization grievously.

2. He may be operating from his fearful Child ego state, in which he feels very insecure. His "thinking" here is that if he can just get everything in writing, when the going gets rough he can prove he was not at fault.

3. He may not realize there is any other way to run things. When I was dean of a college, a professor who had spent most of his working life in a memo-ridden organization was puzzled when I asked him why he hadn't done something I had asked him to do. "I know you mentioned doing it," he said, "but since you didn't put it in writing, I didn't think you meant it."

An administrator at another university sent his professors so many controlling and upsetting memos, they stopped going to their mailboxes before teaching a class because the memos interfered with their concentration. This was only a partial solution, because the professors knew the memos were there, ticking away like time bombs. The administrator prided himself on his organizational ability and could be found almost any time of the day in his office, busily composing memos.

Analyze your written communication with others. Strive for Adult-to-Adult transactions. Avoid sending Critical Parent memos that try to control the behavior of others. Remember that the Adult ego state is interested in controlling *results*, not people.

A Pre-recorded Conversation

Helen and Joe are talking at the office. They are close to a serious disagreement. Neither one knows how they got into this discussion, nor why it's turning out the way it is. Neither is really aware that the way they handle this discussion, plus the thousands like it they have every week, determines to a great extent how successful their careers will be.

The reason Helen and Joe aren't getting along is that they, like Sam and Mr. Post, both assume communication is simple. Two people merely talk to each other, a process they think is rational and logical. In business college they learned to raise their hand dutifully and state that the answer to the business problem they were studying was "a problem in communication." This usually brought a wise smile from the professor, a nod of approval, and that was that. "Communication" is one of the great buzz words on campus, but it is seldom, if ever, analyzed. Students are not taught *how* to communicate.

Real communication is so difficult that many people never engage in it. They merely talk at each other. When they get together, their memorized statements pass each other like ships in the night. It could be said of such conversations, "This program has been prerecorded."

Thousands of meetings take place every day in organizations where people talk at each other and no one knows what the others really think, feel, or mean. Someone presents a problem in the form of a recorded message, such as: "We've got too much dead wood around here" or "You guys aren't selling hard enough" or "We've got to buckle down" or "We've got to cut expenses."

Often the recorded message compares the business problem with end runs in football, or home runs, or sinking ships, or some other vivid metaphor that further disguises the problem. A recorded announcement out of touch with reality gains nothing in clarity when the problem is compared to the third-quarter play in the last Ohio State game.

Everyone tunes out the recorded messages much the same as you tune out conversations on the weather, unless the recorded announcement is of a personal nature, such as: "Why don't you make more calls?" directed to a particular salesman in a sales meeting. The salesman may respond with recorded feelings from his fearful Child ego state, and once again, very little communication leading to problem-solving has taken place. Nothing has been communicated other than a paralyzing threat. There is no interchange of ideas. No planning has been done. Nothing has been activated other than boredom in some cases, and hostility or despair in others.

Watch Out for the One-Down Feeling

Alfred Adler believed that feelings of inferiority were apparent universally, and Thomas Harris says the universality of the I'm Not OK position is a reasonable deduction.* This means when we're transacting with another person, it's very likely we feel one-down. And of course, it follows that if we feel one-down, we naturally consider the other person one-up. But—and this is important—if two people are transacting, there is a good chance that *both* feel one-down and both think the other is one-up. What happens? Neither person will treat the Not OKness in the other because he thinks the other is already OK and it is he, himself, who needs help, understanding, and good strokes. Both parties may ignore the needs of the other. They may even, because they think the other person is one-up on them, kid, tease, or otherwise discount the person.

It's easy to forget about the one-down feeling, or the Not OK Child, especially when your best friend asks for your frank opinion on whether or not he or she needs to lose weight, or your boss asks for your objective appraisal of his or her idea. That's why criticism,

*I'm OK—You're OK; Avon edition, p. 67.

even when asked for, has to be given the way porcupines are supposed to make love—very carefully. I learned this—in fact, you might say I internalized it—quite a few years ago when I was teaching in the psychology department of a university. The head of the department, whose doctorate was in the behavioral sciences, asked me to tell him exactly what I thought of his course syllabus. I was not worried about his reaction to my unfavorable opinion because, after all, he was trained to handle negative feedback; he was an "expert in human relations." He fired me on the spot.

Rules for Good Communication

Good communication requires that, in addition to Creative Listening, we remember and practice the following:

1. All of us have a need to feel good about ourselves. This is what people are up to most of the time. We have doubts about our adequacies and ability to cope. We bring these doubts to all transactions with others. For good communication to take place, you must help others to feel OK about themselves.

2. Don't invite the other person to feel Not OK. This may cause anger and aggression. When we feel Not OK we are not listening; we're defending ourselves.

3. Learn to identify the ego state you are in and the ego state of the one you're talking to.

4. If the other person is in his Critical Parent or Not OK Child ego state, practice mental and verbal "whittling." Soothe him with quiet words. Make no controversial statements. Listen carefully to spot the moment the person shifts to his Adult. There is a good chance he will calm down, stop quoting rules and regulations, and in his Adult ego state, say, "Maybe we can solve this." This will not happen unless you keep *your* Adult firmly in charge.

5. Enter the world of the person or group you're talking to. You then share, in common, the world of another. You perceive as others perceive, and this is what "communion" and communica-

tion are all about. On a very practical level, if Mr. Post, in the Dashman case, had not been so busy playing the role of the executive, he might have *listened* to the men in the field and *looked* at purchasing problems as they did.

6. Stroking improves communication. When you give recognition and encouragement, you make it safer for others to explore the real meaning of your conversation. They can drop their defenses and consider your viewpoint.

A Human Relationship

Roger had been with his company for twenty years, having joined it fresh out of high school. After five promotions, he headed the accounting department and reported directly to the financial vice president.

Roger was a quiet man with an excellent attitude toward his work. When there was extra work or time was short, you could always count on him. After long years of working during the day and going to school at night, he received his master's degree in accounting. Many people believed Roger would take over as financial vice president in several years when the current financial V.P. retired.

And then something happened. Everyone working in Roger's department noticed it, and so did Roger's boss, the financial vice president. Roger's attitude and personality seemed to change almost overnight. He became snappish and testy with the people under him in his department. He missed a great deal of time at work and gave no reason for his absence.

This dragged on for four months, with Roger's behavior getting worse by the week. The ending could have been disastrous for Roger. If his boss had handled the situation from his Critical Parent, called Roger in and chewed him out with memorized statements about right and wrong, Roger, under great strain and feeling Not OK about himself, would probably have quit.

Roger's boss might have repeated the tape used by an executive I know in New York whose analysis of most problems begins and ends with: "Business is business." Or, in his Not OK Child, Roger's boss might have felt Roger was defying him, and his Child's angry feelings might have required that he fire Roger.

But he realized that his job, as financial vice president, of accounting for the company's finances was only part of his work. The other part was human resource accounting and included understanding the men and women who worked for him, not only because it was the human thing to do, but also because it made good financial sense.

His Adult knew he must find out more about the situation. He must have more data before a decision could be reached; so he took Roger out to dinner. He always tried to set a climate where people could talk to him. He asked Roger what was wrong and whether he could help. Roger sensed his boss was actually *listening* to him and wanted to be supportive; so he opened up and disclosed his problem.

Roger's son was in trouble on a drug charge. When Roger first heard about it, he not only suffered for his son, but felt ashamed and disgraced and wanted no one to know. His absences had been for meetings with the lawyer, the judge, and later to enter his son in a rehabilitation program.

The financial v.p. gave Roger warm positive strokes. Just listening was a big stroke; but in addition, his Nurturing Parent assured Roger how highly the company valued him and that having a son in trouble on a drug charge had nothing to do with Roger's worth to the company. He pledged his support and the support of the company during Roger's trying time.

Thanks to a boss who could choose the ego state he would operate in, Roger straightened out and once again became a productive human being. He was able to pass on the understanding his boss had given him to help his son back to health.

Roger's boss is a therapeutic force. By operating in his Adult and Nurturing Parent, he helps others, he helps his company, and he also makes his own existence meaningful. Martin Buber was talking about teachers, but he could have been referring to an executive, a manager, or a parent when he said: "He feels that he may trust this man, that this man is not making a business out of him, but is taking part in his life, accepting him before desiring to influence him."*

Why J.B. Can't Exercise His Authority

J.B. is not like Roger's boss. He's younger and partway up the corporate ladder, but he probably won't get very far. Four people report to him, and three of them disregard half his instructions, loaf on the job, and arrange their work so that much of it is on undeserved overtime.

If J.B. were operating in his Adult, he would have a talk with the three employees, lay out guidelines, and tell them calmly the penalty for violating his instructions. After observing their behavior and attitude carefully, he would, if they continued their losing ways, dismiss them.

Unfortunately for J.B. and his organization, he can't observe fellow workers from his Adult ego state. His Child, because of experiences in his early life, avoids friction at all costs. The minute his Adult starts thinking he should take action, an automatic relay cuts in with the message: "Don't cause trouble. Don't stir things up or you'll be sorry." He can't even calmly tell his secretary that he wants her to arrive at work on time and not spend the first thirty minutes at the coffee shop.

J.B. has learned from long experience that the slightest conflict with another triggers deep feelings of Not OKness within him that he can't handle. He needs to free his Adult. He must tell himself that it's OK to tell others what to do, it's O.K. if everyone doesn't love him all the time. He needs to give himself permission to

*Martin Buber, *Between Man and Man* (New York: Macmillan, 1965), p. 106.

disagree with others. In his case, since his feelings are deep and pervasive, it would probably help him to join a TA group. He could then *sense* his own feelings, and the TA therapist, presuming he is qualified, could give him powerful permission to disobey the Parent tapes that threaten his Child.

If it sounds unbusinesslike to talk about J.B. needing permission to assert his authority in an Adult fashion, remember it's much more unproductive to fire people from the Critical Parent or hang on to people who should be dismissed because the Child is afraid of controversy. What *is* unbusinesslike and unproductive is to assume that there is no way to change the way you are.

Ten Principles for Working with Others

1. Don't expect people to be 100 percent rational and reasonable. We are not always logical. In the Parent ego state we may mouth platitudes. In the Child ego state we may feel bad about ourselves and be quick to anger.

2. Build others' self-esteem as much as possible. The universal human malady is Not OKness. When you hear Not OKness in others, ignore their words and talk to their inner Child.

3. Treat each person as unique. Give individual attention at every opportunity.

4. Strive for Adult-to-Adult transactions. Describe reality without making others feel bad about themselves. Attack the problem, not the personality.

5. Be aware of the pitfalls of power. The Parent ego state controls people with memos, directives, rules, bureaucratic procedures, and red tape. The Adult aims to control *results,* not *people.*

6. To receive accurate feedback on your environment, stay out of your Critical Parent and Not OK Child states. No one brings unfavorable, though realistic, news to a leader who responds with disapproval, anger, or fear.

7. When you're in charge, explain the overall goals so that everyone feels a part of the whole.

8. Tell people *what* is expected of them, but as far as possible, leave the *how* to them. This satisfies the inner Child's need for both security and freedom, and it permits the Adult to function.

9. Encourage the creativity of the Natural Child in others. Winners grow in a climate where their Natural Child and Adult ego states are allowed to work together.

10. Remember, whether giving or receiving orders, many of us resent authority. Don't trigger the Not OK Child in others and don't let yours get hooked.

8

A New Way to Solve Problems

It is generally believed that you're either born smart or not, and that's all there is to it; but this is not true, because you can improve your problem-solving ability and when you do, you become smarter. You make better decisions and the quality of your life is enhanced. (I'm not talking about IQ here because in education and psychology we don't really know what IQ is, except that it is what an IQ test measures, but we do know from hard educational research that there is no correlation between a person's IQ and his creativity. Along that line, I agree with Einstein that imagination is much more important than knowledge.)

The Einstellung Effect

By early adolescence most of us have a set way we solve each problem we encounter. The "solution routes" in our mind become so fixed and unchanging that our approach to problems does not so much resemble "thinking" as stimulus and immediate, unthinking response. This phenomenon is so common it has a name—the Einstellung effect. The original experiments on "mental sets" took place in Germany, and *Einstellung* is the German word for "set."

"Mental set" simply means that when it comes to many of the

problems we face in life, we don't really "think" about them in a creative way but refuse to enter the problem and *look around* at all. We "solve" it with an old solution that has already formed a comfortable pathway in our mind. Real thinking is terribly uncomfortable and anxiety-producing for many people, and they have been taught nothing regarding how to go about it.

Morton Hunt, in his excellent book *The Thinking Animal*, gives a good example illustrating "mental set." Students were shown into a room containing a bucket of dirty water, rope, wire, tools, and an open pipe anchored to the floor with Ping-Pong balls at the bottom. The pipe was too deep for them to reach the Ping-Pong balls, and the students were told to use anything in the room to get the balls out. It didn't take them too long to see that they could pour the dirty water from the bucket into the pipe to float the balls to the top. Then another group of students was shown the same setup with exactly the same tools, except that this time the water was clean ice water in a pitcher on a table set with a white tablecloth and crystal goblets. It took the second group of students much longer to figure out how to get the Ping-Pong balls out because they had a mental set: They saw the pitcher of water only for drinking, and not for pouring down an open pipe.*

The purpose of brainstorming, a technique in wide use today, is to overcome "mental sets." Each member of a group employing brainstorming is expected to come up with the most outlandish ideas he can think of and in this way "jump" outside the preformed pathways in his mind. There is to be no criticism of any idea, as this would cause the members to retreat to the same old pathways of "thinking." Some very creative solutions are discovered this way.

---

*M. Hunt, *The Thinking Animal* (Boston: Little, Brown, 1964), p. 205. ·

Characteristics of Good Problem-Solvers

A good problem-solver is flexible. He could be compared with a good quarterback who, when he finds he can't move his team off tackle, tries an end-run, and when that doesn't work, goes to the air. Good problem-solvers are flexible, but you have to go deeper than that and ask the questions: Why are some people flexible and others rigid? Why do some people make one good decision after another, while others close off all their options with one unwise decision after another? What is it that allows some people to take a problem, toy with it, turn it over and over, change direction and continue searching? (Not so incidentally, Einstein, when asked how he made his discoveries, replied, "I grope.") What causes others to snap to an immediate decision, and then defend it in the face of evidence to the contrary?

Those Damned Circles and Ovals

An interesting experiment on difficult differentiations was carried out by the famous Russian physiologist Ivan Pavlov over forty years ago. He would teach a dog that whenever he saw a circle he would get food, but would get nothing when he saw an oval. Then Pavlov made the ovals appear more and more like circles so the dog couldn't differentiate between the two. After a number of days of this, the dog started running in circles, howling and displaying what could be labeled neurosis. The decisions were just too difficult to make.

Similar experiments have been conducted on other animals. In one, when the animal hears a certain tone and opens a box, he gets food; a different tone means he gets a shock when he opens the box. Then the tones are made to sound almost alike, and again, the animal shows signs of extreme agitation.

I first heard of these experiments a number of years ago, but I've always remembered them because they are similar to what you and

I put up with every day of our life. We face anguishing decisions, where the tones sound alike and the circles look like ovals:

> Should we decide on the new job or keep the old one?
> Should we decide to get more education or look harder for a job?
> Should we sell the house and move to another neighborhood?
> Should we accept the promotion and move or not?
> Should we send our child to a different school?
> Should we back our child at school, or is the teacher right?
> Should we have the operation or take our chances without it?
> Should we marry him (or her) or would we be better off single?
> Should we have another child?
> Should we get a divorce, or is it better to stay married?
> Should we start that new business, or is it better to stay with the organization?

We must make most of our decisions under conditions of great uncertainty, and it is this fact that causes many people to jump at answers to avoid the pain.

It's Both a Cat and a Dog

Some people simply can't tolerate ambiguity; they can't hold conflicting ideas in their mind at the same time. They can't be comfortable with new concepts and ideas. In an interesting experiment,* people are shown a series of pictures, one at a time. The first picture is clearly a dog, then each successive picture gradually and almost imperceptibly changes so that in the middle of the series, the picture the subject is shown is really half dog and half cat. Many people continue calling the pictures "dog" even after the halfway mark, where cat characteristics predominate. It seems that many cannot think "half dog, half cat," and some continue to say

*Else Frenkel-Brunswik, "Intolerance of Ambiguity as an Emotional and Perceptual Personality Variable," *Journal of Personality* (1949), 18:108–143.

"dog" even after the picture obviously shows a cat. These unlucky people are imprisoned in their original perception, much as if a part of their thinking apparatus had been destroyed. They can't or won't change their minds; they can't perceive reality.

The Inner Child and Problem-Solving

It is the fearful Child within that demands immediate closure on any problem it encounters. It feels comfortable only with certainty. It has even been trained this way by our institutions. Some teachers demand pat answers, given within a short time span. Imagine requiring a fast answer from your doctor, dentist, lawyer, mechanic, with no consultation of books or colleagues allowed, nor stopping to think about it permitted. Under our present educational system, actual *thinking*—using the mind to experiment, "play" with the question, explore, ask foolish questions, brainstorm, and freewheel—is discouraged. Our religious institutions also discourage questions by the young, as if God must be protected from creative inquiry. Often the youngster who brings home the best grades is the tight-lipped, seldom smiling, rigid little person who uses his entire mental energy in figuring out what will please the teacher. Observing this overtrained little person, you see why studies show there is no correlation between IQ and creativity. This training is internalized and the Critical Parent within demands perfection of the personality, telling it to hurry up, insisting that the right decision be made even when it is impossible to tell the circles from the ovals.

Effective problem-solvers operate from their Adult, consult appropriate Parent tapes, and sometimes get a strong assist from the creative, intuitive part of their OK Child. The OK Child, along with Adult insight, often sees the humor in a situation. It can be detached from the sense of strain and tension and perceive that the picture is, in reality, half dog and half cat.

A spirit of play often helps greatly in solving problems. It might help you to remember the famous remark of the Nobel Prize-winning Danish physicist Niels Bohr, who, when a graduate student complained there was too much horseplay and joking in Bohr's laboratory, replied, "But there are some things so important that one can only joke about them."

Tentare

The Adult, with his fearful and impulsive Not OK Child under control, can be tentative; *tentare* is Latin for "to try on for fit," and this is what the Adult does. The Adult lowers anxiety and considers the solution. He makes statements such as:

"Let's see if we can get more facts."
"I may be wrong, so I'm going to delay as long as possible."
"I'd like to sleep on it."
"They look similar, but there's a fine difference."
"That's a good idea; it just might work."
"I changed my mind."
"Can we improve on this?"
"I didn't think of that."
"I'd like to correct what I said earlier."

It's not the Adult in control of the decision-making process if you hear statements such as:

"There's no doubt about it."
"There's only one thing to do." (There are usually many options.)
"I know I'm right."
"I don't want to hear any more about it."
"It's a sure way to make a killing."
"To hell with it—what can we lose?"

The "Don't Think" Injunction and Problem-Solving

Many well-meaning parents teach their children they shouldn't think for themselves. When the child enters school this is sometimes reinforced by teachers who teach the child everything but the joy and wonder of using his brain to think his own way through life. (See Chapter 12: Raising OK Children.)

The parents give their child an injunction that plainly says, "Don't think," when they supervise and criticize his every move. The child matures with no problem-solving experience. After little Morris, for the thousandth time, is told he put on the wrong pants, plays with the wrong kids, eats the wrong foods, says the wrong words, and has outlandish ideas, it isn't surprising that little Morris concludes that to get along in his household he had better stop making any decisions at all and wait to be told what to do.

Many parental injunctions are given nonverbally by a look of disapproval, or indirectly through jests and insinuations. Claude Steiner says: "The injunction . . . is always a prohibition or an inhibition of the free behavior of the child. . . . Injunctions vary in range, intensity, area of restriction, and malignancy. Some injunctions affect a very small range of behavior, such as 'don't sing,' or 'don't laugh loudly,' or 'don't eat too many sweets.' Others are extremely comprehensive in range, such as 'don't be happy,' 'don't think,' or 'don't do anything.' "*

Morris is indoctrinated through childhood to "Do what I tell you to do when I tell you to do it, and stop when I say so." And then the day he leaves for college or goes out to get a job, he is sent off with the expectation that now that he's on his own he will make wise decisions.

Morris was raised on a "Don't think" injunction. He learned that the only way to please his mother was to wait for her specific

*C. Steiner, *Games Alcoholics Play,* (New York: Grove Press, 1971); Ballantine edition, p. 35. Also on injunctions see C. Steiner, *Scripts People Live* (New York: Grove Press, 1974), p. 101 and R. Goulding and M. Goulding, *Transactional Analysis Journal* Jan. 1976, "Injunctions, Decisions, and Redecisions)," p 41.

instructions. He stopped thinking on his own. When he got up in the morning he waited for his mother to tell him what to wear.

Morris's father showed him how to get along with his mother. Morris's mother, being consistent, not only wanted a son who wouldn't think for himself, but had chosen a husband who wouldn't think for himself either. So Morris's father provided a living example. He showed his son how to get along by letting his mother do all the thinking, make all the decisions. Now Morris is in his thirties; his boss may fire him because Morris can't make decisions for himself.

The injunction we receive from parents and have reinforced by some teachers: "Don't think," is a hard spell to break and may account for the way we let the "experts" think for us. To help my students break this spell I sometimes gave a vague assignment for a term paper, such as: "Do something that will cause you to grow as a human being, and give me some kind of record of what you have done at the end of the term." I tell them I will accept anything that shows thought. Some students are delighted with this kind of assignment and dig in with relish. They rejoice in escaping the Mickey Mouse assignment that weighs in at a quarter of a pound, material copied from other sources.

But the students with a "Don't think" injunction are at first stunned and then outraged. What kind of instructions are those for a term assignment? You can see and hear them refusing to think. They ask how long should the paper be, what should it *really* be on, what do I mean by "some kind of record," when am I going to tell them what to do?

The cry of those under a "Don't think" injunction is: "We don't understand what you want," but what they really mean is: "What do you mean, asking us to think for ourselves? That's not fair."

Problems Present a Threat

Gordon, a family friend for many years, received an excellent offer from a manufacturing company in Southern California. He always wanted to live there; so he quit his job in New York and moved to the West Coast. He and his wife purchased a home, settled the children in school, and started enjoying their new life.

Everything was fine for six months until a merger was announced; Gordon's company had been taken over by a larger company. Everyone in the smaller company felt insecure, and sure enough, one Friday afternoon Gordon was called into his boss's office and released from his job.

Gordon panicked and his fearful Child took over. He told me later: "The day I was fired I stopped thinking. I was in a strange city with a wife and three children where we had not yet learned our way around the streets, let alone made any friends or business connections. I had a large savings account, but all I could think of was running back as fast as I could to my old job. I was scared. My feelings took over completely and nothing entered my mind but trying to recapture as quickly as possible a feeling of security."

Gordon called his previous boss in New York three days after he was released from his West Coast job. Since they had worked well together, his boss wanted him back; so after much trouble and expense, Gordon sold his house and once again moved across country, this time from West to East.

Gordon admitted later he regretted not looking for another job on the West Coast after he got squeezed out in the merger. "Here I was," he said, "all settled in a house, with the children in school, and a good savings account. There was no reason to panic. My wife and I both loved the area and had wanted to live there all our lives; we still do. Yet all I could feel was fear and came running back to my old job in New York as fast as possible."

This happens to people when they let their Child take over. The sequence goes like this:

1. We perceive a problem.

2. The problem presents a threat of failure.

3. We allow our fearful Child to take over and focus on the threat.

4. With the fearful Child in charge, the Adult is unable to come up with alternate solutions.

5. The problem is "solved" by the Child.

There's Much More to Problem-Solving than Optimism

Joe Elkhart is forty-three. His problem is the same as that of thousands of other men and women. Unlike Ben, who was passed over for the presidency, Joe may be passed over at a lower level or he might even be fired. After seventeen years with the company, he now sees signs that tell him he has gone as far as he can go. As I said in Chapter 6, organizations are pyramids. Academicians flirt with other forms of organization, such as circular ones with power flowing out from a central core, or linear ones with everyone equal. These organizational structures look nice on a blackboard and make good final-exam questions. But in the real world, organizations are pyramids with many at the bottom, fewer supervisors, even fewer in middle management, and only several at the top. There is only one corporate president and one chairman of the board.

Good men and women can be either pushed off the pyramid or entombed at lower levels. There are just so many openings and the closer you get to the top, the fewer positions there are for people to move up to.

Joe possesses all the qualifications for a higher-level position, but he knows he has gone as far as he can. The thought makes him miserable. It eats on him night and day. He's as good as the men and women above him in the hierarchy. He's probably smarter than the president. But somewhere along the line, fate handed Joe a bad card. It had nothing to do with skill or intelligence. Often the bad card is called politics. Sometimes it's a merger, or just a dead-end job. And occasionally there is no reason.

There might be three good persons ready for the next step up. All three have equal skills and are equally liked. One has to be chosen and two have to stand still. Management in these situations has all the logical analysis of a crap shot. As one honest vice president humorously put it, "When we have two equally skilled persons to consider for one opening, we do it the scientific way. We flip a coin."

Joe came to a dead end in middle management. It also happens higher up the pyramid; it's common even on the vice-presidential level. *Fortune* magazine carried an article about the problem of the passed-over vice presidents (see Chapter 6). A vice president who has been accustomed to climbing up the pyramid all his life is devastated when he's passed over and someone else gets the job. Reactions range from despondency to depression to suicide.

Joe operates in his Adult most of the time when dealing with other people at work, but he operates in his Child ego state when thinking about his career. Joe's Child was raised to believe that if you work long and hard and are loyal and true, you will automatically succeed in a big way; and if you don't make it, you aren't thinking right. This oversimplified idea results in Not OK feelings in many people, especially during middle age. It is spread by some people who forget they not only "thought right," but had a great deal of good fortune along the way. Not a month goes by that I don't hear from one of my older students or clients something to the effect, "I don't know where I went wrong. I have not succeeded as well as some others. I guess I don't think right."

Being optimistic is a good idea, but the Child forgets there's a lot more to problem-solving than that. Aside from resulting in Not OK feelings when everything doesn't go right, oversimplified Child expectations prevent preparation for a rainy day. It's almost part of Joe's religion that there won't be any rainy days. During his seventeen years with his organization, Joe never really, in his Adult, considered his existential problems, how he would survive financially and psychologically if for some reason he lost his job. He vaguely felt this was negative thinking. In all his years of college, not one professor mentioned that the structure of the pyramid made the odds overwhelmingly against his ever becoming a vice president, let alone the number-one man. He was taught on the rosy, but unrealistic, assumption that life would be like a jet speeding down the runway, lifting and climbing toward the sun. "Onward and Upward" was the motto of the business school Joe attended. Just "think right," work hard, and all your problems will be solved.

Not just Joe, but all of us need to develop options early in our lives. We need other avenues and choices open to us. Sometimes we get stuck in organizations, sometimes we decide in middle life we don't like what we're doing, sometimes we are forced into retirement when we'd still like to be active and productive.

I live in Florida, where people come to retire. Many men and women who have been active all their lives find retirement not to their taste. They wither under forced inactivity and life grows dull. Some of these people sit in a rocker, facing backward toward the past, and grow old before their time. Others become active again and find new zest in their lives. One man who comes to mind as I write this worked for a large retailing company in Pennsylvania and went to school at night to earn his bachelor's degree. He then re-enrolled in night school and went through two more years of drudgery to get his master's degree. He told me later, "I really don't know why I went back to school to get a master's degree at night. I had a wife and child and was under no pressure from my company to get a graduate degree, but I had a faint idea that someday I might like to teach." His faint idea became a reality thirty years later. When he was sixty-eight years old I hired him as a full-time faculty member of the university where I was dean. With his experience, wisdom, and knowledge, he was one of our most valuable assets. His going to night school to earn a graduate degree is one of the options I'm talking about when I say that Joe, and all the rest of us, need to develop other choices in our life whenever possible.

Playing "I've Got a Secret" to Solve Investment Problems

Neil and Grace live in an apartment in a suburb of New York. Both have held executive jobs in the city for over twenty years. They have no children. They have never had a major illness. With their combined incomes they should be well off. They can live on less than half their income after taxes. But they have money problems; retirement is coming up in a few years and they have very little savings. They lost thousands of dollars over the years in foolish investments. Neil and Grace are smarter than average. They earn their money in their Adult, but invest it in their Child ego state.

They play an investment game I call "I've Got a Secret." This game begins with someone coming on with strong Parent tapes and telling an overanxious Neil and Grace that he is a professional money manager and has a secret way to make money fast. He tells them to put their money in ———— (fill in the blank, depending on the latest national get-rich-quick fad).

If they were operating in their Adult, Neil and Grace would see through the unending schemes, forecasts, and promises. But there are two things they have a taboo against discussing seriously: sex and money. Whenever they discuss either, they revert to their Child. They even talk about "playing the market," or taking a "fling" in Arizona real estate. Their mental tape collection on investments is a dilly. Some of their hit tunes include:

"What Can We Lose?"
"Nothing Ventured, Nothing Gained."
"You've Got to Trust Somebody."
"Sooner or Later We'll Hit It Big."
"This Is a Chance in a Million."
"What the Hell, It's Only Money."

These tapes lost them money on every investment fad of the fifties, sixties, and seventies. They bought every bubble their investment "advisor" came up with. Every bubble burst. To name a few:

The Uranium Craze of the Fifties
The Go-Go Funds
The Hedge Funds
The Hot New Issues
The Concept Stocks
The Fast Growth Stocks
The Performance Funds

Neil and Grace lost more than their standard amount on a performance fund. They met an expert "I've Got A Secret" player at their country club. He was all dressed up in a good suit and expensive tie and had appeared often on the local stock market channel predicting market moves and giving out "professional" advice that would cause people who really made money in the market to double up in laughter. As Neil and Grace said, "He must know what he is doing because, after all, he owns a jet that flies him all over the country."

He showed Neil and Grace his jet. He explained to them that it allowed him to learn secrets faster than anyone else. While other secret investment hunters were waiting around commercial airports, he was already on the scene.

Other "I've Got a Secret" players joined Neil and Grace. They all agreed: "How can you lose with a guy who handles millions of dollars and flies around the country in his own jet finding investment opportunities?"

The expert and his jet stayed in the air until the market break of 1973–74. The jet made its last landing in November of 1974. The fund came down earlier. The shares that Neil and Grace bought for fifty-five dollars a share are now selling for pennies.

"Looking for Baruch" Is Easier than Adult Decision-Making

When Neil and Grace aren't playing "I've Got a Secret," they play what I call "Looking for Bernard Baruch,"* in the undying hope that at last they have found a broker who will make them rich. In this version, Neil and Grace are "tipped" on a high flier by the broker they chose in their child ego state, who knows little about investments and no more about the future than anyone else. The opening move begins with the broker conjuring up a picture of Santa coming down the chimney with his bag full of winnings.

"Have you got a minute, Neil?" the broker whispers into the phone. Neil listens, then plays his standard tapes for Grace: "What the hell, let's take a flier. A stopped clock is right twice a day. What can we lose? You only go around once. It's only money." Grace, pleased with Neil's "analysis" and the way he's moving things along, replies with: "Yes, sooner or later we'll hit it big."

Joe, the broker, says he has no idea what the stock might do (strict compliance with the New York Stock Exchange rule), but . . . off the record, he doesn't see how they can miss quadrupling their money. So they "take a fling" again.

Six months later Neil and Grace call Joe the broker to sell their stock and take their loss. Joe plays his recorded announcements: "Times change" and "If it hadn't been for ———" (again, fill in the blank with any of the hundreds of things that can happen in a six-month period—a market crash, a dollar devaluation, a presidential assassination, war).

When Neil and Grace think about their investment decisions, which is seldom, they conclude they're not smart enough to make money. The truth is they're smart enough; besides, you don't have to be smart to be rich. What you need is iron control of your Child's belief in Santa Claus and the Good Fairy. The Child wants something for nothing; it's greedy and impatient. It craves excitement

---

*Adviser to Presidents of the United States, one of the few persons to make a fortune speculating in the stock market—and keep it.

and recognition. It needs the positive strokes that come from winning. It sometimes relishes even the punishing negative strokes that come with losing.

Neil and Grace don't need a more intelligent Adult ego state; they need to allow their Adult to operate. They must learn to recognize their Child and decide it won't make investment decisions for them.

Neil and Grace are good examples of people who wander through their lives "looking for the expert." I used a financial example because so many people are interested in investing, and there are so many "experts" giving advice they hope will hook the Child expectations of others. But examples of Child expectations overriding Adult knowledge abound in all areas of life. We think that somewhere, somehow, there is an expert who can solve our problem perfectly for us if we can just find him. If we but knew, we are our own expert. We can solve our own problems better than anyone. We can gather our own information, dig out our own facts, weigh probabilities ourselves. We must ignore the Parent tape if it says, "You're not smart enough to solve this. Don't think about it." We must also monitor the uneasiness and uncertainty of the Child within us. If the Child expects a perfect or an easy solution, these expectations must be checked by our Adult. It must also be remembered that to stand still and do nothing is a decision in itself, and sometimes the one carrying the most risk.

"Discounting" in Problem-Solving

Jacqui Schiff, a leading TA theorist and a pioneer in the field, has had near miraculous results re-Parenting schizophrenics. Her work is with seriously disturbed people; however, after talking with her at length about her Discounting theory, she and I agreed it might very well give valuable insights in problem-solving to so-called normal people.

Discounting, according to Ms. Schiff, is an internal mechanism which involves people minimizing or ignoring some aspect of themselves, others, or the reality of a situation. She says there are four different mechanisms people use in discounting, and they are listed in order, with the most serious discounting mechanism first.

On Level Number One, Ms. Schiff says that people discount the problem itself and set it up so the problem, to them, doesn't even *exist.* She uses the example of parents taking sleeping pills so they won't hear the baby crying, or shutting him off alone so he won't disturb them. On this level of problem-solving, people protect themselves from even knowing the problem exists.

On Level Number Two, Ms. Schiff says that people are aware of the problem, but discount its *significance.* To continue the example of the crying baby, she says on this level the people hear the baby crying (they are aware of the problem), but they dismiss it with reasons they find acceptable to themselves and which require no action on their part. They say that all babies cry, or that he's merely exercising his lungs. While Ms. Schiff was talking about this type of discounting, I couldn't help thinking about a man I knew who was fired from a high-paying job, and, although he had to take another one at half the pay, he and his wife kept on living at their previous level of expenditure, denying the significance of their problem right up until their world collapsed.

On Level Number Three, people discount the *solvability* of a problem. Ms. Schiff says that on this level people see the problem, but they say there is nothing they can do to solve it. They hear the baby crying, but say he always cries and there is nothing they can do to make him stop. Actually, he might be crying because he has an earache and needs treatment. On this level, at least people are aware of the problem and its significance, unlike the two previous discounting mechanisms. Ms. Schiff says that many people discount the solvability of a problem and don't look at all the possible solutions to a situation. However, this level of discounting is less serious because people may get suggestions from others on how to solve their problem.

On Level Number Four of discounting, a person discounts *him-*

self. The baby cries, and the mother says, "When the baby cries, I get so nervous that I can't do anything right." Another example Ms. Schiff related was that of a mother who came to her and said she couldn't get her eight-year-old son to turn off the television set because her husband wouldn't back her up. Ms. Schiff analyzes the interesting ways in which this mother discounts both herself and the solvability of the problem: The eight-year-old is incorrigible (probably not true); the mother is so inadequate she can't turn off the television set (probably not true); the husband is so powerful he has control over the television set, even in his absence (probably not true).*

The Adult, in problem-solving, takes charge and says in effect, "This is my problem; it's an important one, and no one is as interested in the outcome as I am. I will learn what is necessary to come to a wise decision." One of the purposes of this book is to help busy, intelligent people to sort out their three selves so they can calmly say, when confronted by life's problems, "I trust myself."

Summary: Boswell's Rules for Problem-Solving

Once the Adult is in charge of our personality, we become effective in that important human activity—problem-solving. Here are some rules I've formulated and tested for effective and efficient problem-solving:

1. Make certain you identify and define the problem *precisely.* State the problem in as few words as possible.

2. In the initial stages of problem-solving or decision-making, establish a climate of play wherein the consequences of "wrong thinking" are minimal.

3. In the play stage, brainstorm your problem. To brainstorm, turn off the Critical Parent tapes, quit playing "Ain't It Awful,"

---

*Permission granted by Jacqui Schiff and Aaron Schiff in conversation with the author.

merely repeating the problem over and over. Strive for alternate solutions, no matter how wild. Do not criticize the solutions; allow the mind to freewheel. Remember *tentare;* try out and reject hypotheses. Have no concern at this stage with convention or what people think.

4. Get off "hurry-up" time (see Chapter 9). Hurry-up time does not allow proper scanning of the environment. Effective people allot more time than necessary to get a job done or a problem solved because they know the "unexpected" delays should be expected.

5. Do not allow the Critical Parent to pressure you toward a solution. You can't process information efficiently under pressure. Jerome Bruner of Harvard says: "One state in which information is least useful is that of strong drive and anxiety."*

6. Make certain your goal is problem-solving and not anxiety-reduction. The girl who marries the first man who proposes reduces her anxiety, but often increases her problems. The same is true of a person who takes the first job that comes along.

7. With the Adult firmly in charge, weigh the risk/reward ratio. The Not OK Child takes great risks to achieve small rewards because any reward makes it feel better about itself. The fearful Child avoids risk altogether, even where the reward might be great. The Adult objectively computes probabilities.

8. Avoid mental sets. This is caused by: *(a)* Parent tapes which try to fit old solutions onto new problems, and *(b)* Child feelings that focus on the threat of failure, causing tunnel vision.

9. With important and long-range decisions such as marriage, buying a home, moving to a distant city, the Adult must consult the Child for its *feelings* in the matter. An Adult decision that ignores the needs of the Child is unwise; sooner or later the Child will rebel and subvert it.

10. Problems present a threat of failure, which will cause self-

*Jerome S. Bruner, *Toward a Theory of Instruction* (New York: W. W. Norton & Company, 1966), p. 52.

contempt. The Not OK Child dreads the beating it will take from the Critical Parent if it makes a mistake. ("How could you do such a thing?" "How dumb can you be?" "At this rate you'll be in the poorhouse," etc.) The Adult must give the personality *permission* to make mistakes. It must take charge and turn off the inner "be perfect" voice.

11. Be alert to the "Don't think" injunction. This can cause you to either give up on the problem or jump at an easy answer. Remember, if you *feel* confused, the Child is trying to mess you up. Confusion is a state of mind and not a feeling.

12. Finally, keep cool in a close decision. No matter how smart you are, often the circles and ovals will look alike.

9

How to Beat the Rat Race

Many men and women complain they are caught in a rat race, condemned to never-ending tension, anxiety, and struggle, merely to stay even in life. They say they would like to escape, but don't know how. I'll discuss leaving the "rat race" later in this chapter, but the question must first be answered: Where is the rat race taking place, inside or outside the person?

Unfortunately, many of those who complain about being caught in a tension-filled, anxiety-producing job can't escape even if they change jobs or move to another location, for the reason that they have a rat-race type of personality. The rat race takes place *inside* them, and though it may be reinforced by the kind of work they are in, changing jobs will not help them until they decide to change *themselves.*

You can recognize the rat-race type of personality by the following symptoms:

1. He always has more to do than he can handle. Time is an enemy. His favorite phrases, which he uses over and over, are: "I'm swamped," "This isn't my day," "I'll never catch up," "This place is wild."

2. He has no time for accuracy. He uses the shotgun approach to conversation, hoping he will hit the mark of his idea, but is in

109

such doubt that he fires blast after blast on the same subject. He ends by asking, "Know what I mean?"

3. Because he has no time for deep understanding, his relationships with others are unsatisfactory and incomplete.

4. He is usually preoccupied. One man I know has been too preoccupied to focus on what anyone was saying for the last twenty years.

5. The rat-race personality is addicted to tension. His nervous system feeds on frenzied activity. When things slow down, he activates them by a phone call, meeting, or trip; and thereby brings back the rat race he craves, claiming all the while that it overwhelms him.

Eric Berne mentioned three kinds of time: goal time, clock time, and hurry-up time.* When working under goal time, you decide to work until you have completed a project. Under clock time, you decide to work until a certain hour. Under the influence of hurry-up time, you set unrealistic goals to be accomplished in an unreasonably short time.

Rat-race personalities are usually on hurry-up time. They don't know there is any other way to live. When you tell them work doesn't have to be accompanied by a feeling of tension and effort, they don't know what you're talking about. They believe that life is divided into two distinct categories: stressful work and relaxation. They can't imagine that work can be tension-free.

For these people it's futile to change jobs to escape tension. Wherever they go, they hear the admonitions of the inner voice: "Hurry up, let's go, get more done, do it faster." Even when on vacation, they feel they should "hurry up." They feel uneasy because they haven't organized their vacation better.

The person with a rat-race personality can escape tension not by changing jobs, but by putting his Adult in charge. The Adult knows that the feeling of hurry, tension, and effort is not the effective way to work. It knows these feelings are the result of the

*E. Berne, *What Do You Say After You Say Hello?* Bantam edition, pp. 210–12.

inner Child's trying to please an unreasonable Critical Parent tape. The Adult learns to ignore the tapes and gives *permission* to relax while working. The Adult says, in effect, "You have permission to enjoy work, to do it effectively, and to accomplish a reasonable amount each day."

Only after the Adult has learned to turn off the Critical tapes can it be decided whether the person is indeed caught in a rat race. If the Adult discovers that the entire organization is on hurry-up time, that everyone is overburdened, that all involved are in a state of tension with clenched jaw and tight stomach, then the Adult can gradually take steps to find another job. (Admittedly, this isn't easy, but men and women are doing this increasingly as their Adult decides that life is indeed short.)

Organizations on Hurry-Up Time

Many organizations are on hurry-up time. They have people in charge who are driven to set a hurry-up atmosphere. They rush about in a breathless, tense state. Their work suffers and they themselves suffer. Unfortunately, many employees who don't have the inner compulsion to "hurry up" also suffer. They need the job and have to fit in.

Companies on hurry-up time judge their employees more by how well they play the role of busy executive than by results. You must appear tense, hurried, and under stress. The assumption is that what you are going to do *next* is much more important than what you are doing *now*. The busy executive reminds those talking with him that he's on hurry-up time by chopping off the end of what they say with, "Right . . . Right . . . Right." The "Right," said in a short, explosive manner, means: "Hurry up, get on with your point."

"Hurry up" can best be indulged in by those organizations that were brilliantly set up by genius founders years ago. Markets were captured, assets bought, financing arranged, and rules laid down so the company could operate almost on automatic. The present executives of these companies are little more than maintenance people. There is not much creative they need do; so they rush around acting busy. This provides the illusion of accomplishment and forward progress.

Those on hurry-up time have to do most things twice. After the executive has hurried his caller on the other end of the line by impatiently shouting, "Right" at him five or six times, there is little chance that communication has taken place. This, of course, necessitates another breathless call, and the extra effort heightens the feeling of accomplishment. I know a broadcasting executive with a major network who responds to all stimuli with fevered activity. His phone conversations consist of one or two small ideas delivered at a frantic pace and repeated four times. He doesn't so much see, hear, and experience others as quickly frisk each conversation for either opportunity or threat. He has been known to lose control of his burning activity, place a call to a distant city, tell the answering party that he's too busy to talk, and hang up.

Executives on hurry-up time help the airlines. Long-distance calls, because they are hurried, leave them vaguely uncertain they have communicated. This prompts one of them to suggest they get together. They are already together, of course, when they are on the phone. The "Let's get together" move presents all kinds of wonderful hurry-up activities. There is self-sacrifice implicit in the hurried orders to the secretary and in the race to the airport. No one, but no one, including the Critical Parent tapes in the executive's head, can criticize our warrior as he takes off for the Coast.

One man I used to know works for a publishing firm in New York. He has been on hurry-up time since he started there. This organization works in five-year cycles. It spends five years hurriedly expanding, hiring people, rushing around; then the next five years retrenching, laying people off, cutting costs. It's the only company he's ever worked for, so this man thinks it's normal to be on hurry-up time. Like the man who wore too tight shoes all his life, he doesn't know there's another way. He has no idea that large empires have been built by relaxed people who live in the here and now, concentrate on the matter at hand, enjoy the fleeting moment, and refuse to be rushed.*

If you are on hurry-up time, if your inner Critical Parent will never let you relax, if you must do everything in half the time it takes the rest of us, then forget about beating the rat race unless you learn to tune in to those inner voices and feelings that drive you on.

Maybe It's Your Imagination

Maybe you aren't really in a rat race; you just imagine you are. Perhaps you don't know what the norm is for making a living, and you idealize the other person's occupation. One of the kindest men I ever knew, who treated others as he would be treated, was coaxed away from a lifetime job with a good retirement pension into a higher position in education, and then fired from this position after he had held it less than one year. I ran into Hugh on campus one day and he said, "Nelson, this is the second time I have been betrayed by a university. I was talking with my wife last night, and I think I'm going to get out of the rat race and go into business."

Those of you in education may not see any humor in Hugh's remarks; and those of you in business will probably laugh that Hugh would think education is a rat race and business is not. The point is, while you want to get out of a rat-race situation, be sure that your expectations are realistic. There are few, if any, trouble-free occupations without bosses who are on Critical Parent tapes some of the time. The most unreasonable human being I ever worked for was the pipe-smoking dean of a college of a well-known

---

*While teaching the behavioral sciences to mostly working men and women, and holding workshops in organizations, I have found nothing that helps people in organizations at all levels, including top executives, as much as TA does. They like TA and quickly grasp P-A-C; racket feelings; life positions; CP and C sabotage of premium time; persecutor, rescuer, and victim roles; hurry-up time; my application of TA to problem-solving, etc.

university, and to top it off, he held his doctorate in the Management of Human Resources. He was (laughter in the wings) an expert in human relations. The professors called him "Dean Mean."

If It's Really a Rat Race, Plan Your Escape

Some people believe they have no wiggling room left in life. Because of accumulated bills, family obligations, and personal pressures, perhaps they can't leave whatever they are doing for a better life. But give this plenty of thought before resigning yourself to this category. You may be like Harper, who despised his job with a broadcasting company in Chicago. He knew what he really wanted, so he quit and moved to southeast Florida. He fell on his face in business and had to beg for his old job back in Chicago. He saved every cent he could and three years later quit his job the second time, moved to Florida again, and sure enough, after one year had to move back to Chicago in the dead of winter. He was lucky enough to secure another job in broadcasting and was promoted to New York. He worked hard for five years, saved up another bundle, quit his job again and, for the third time, moved to southeast Florida. This time it paid off. Today Harper has his own business, his net worth has zoomed to over a million, and everything is going his way.

Should you do the same as Harper? Probably not. But then again, maybe you should. Only you, in your Adult, would know. One thing Harper had against him that maybe you don't is a Not OK Child that would flood him with feelings of self-contempt anytime he failed. After his two defeats in Florida he crawled back to Chicago with every bone in his body aching and every neuron in his head hurting. He told me the only reason he didn't have a full scale "nervous breakdown" each time was that he couldn't afford it.

Don't think everyone with persistence can necessarily do what

Harper did, because the third time he was shot full of luck. But don't let your fearful Child tell you there is no way out for you, either.

If you decide to leave what your Adult—repeat: *Adult*—tells you is a rat race, then plan your escape as carefully as they do in those movies where six characters decide they're going to hold up the local Brink's truck on payday. Plan every move. Place yourself on automatic Adult while you make your plans. If you find yourself saying, "What the hell, we'll just have to take a chance on that aspect of it," pull yourself up short and lay a little more brainpower on the whole scheme. Also, like the famous general, plan what you'll do if you meet defeat. Plan your way around, over, and under the obstacles; and try to identify each and every one of them before you make your move. The big problem in leaving the rat race for greener pastures is the Child within. He'll get spooked pretty fast if things start to go wrong. You'd better plan what you'll do if you get scared as hell, because there's a good chance you will.

You Decide to Stay Put

You may decide to make the best of what you interpret as a bad situation. No one would blame you for doing this. It's a good discipline for all of us to accept, at least temporarily, circumstances that can't be changed and see how well we can handle them. If you think you're in this category now, use your Adult for all it's worth to brainstorm what can be improved and ignore the Parent tape that wants to play "Ain't It Awful" over and over. There's no way your Child can find enjoyment if the Parent keeps telling you it's hopeless.

There's one more thing to weigh in making this decision. Harper, you remember, was a high-roller, accustomed to risk-taking. Another guy—call him Ralph—worked with Harper in New York and disliked the shallowness of his broadcasting job but held on dearly for security's sake. After twenty-five years and four promotions, Ralph was called in one Friday afternoon by a high-priced, low-minded executive and fired on small retirement pay. His parting words to Ralph were: "I can just see you in Florida, patting the hood of a Cadillac as you sell it and having a hell of a time." The executive was wrong. Ralph did not adjust and killed himself six months after he was fired. I think we all know, in our Adult, that staying put is also a decision and may carry as many risks as deciding to leave.

Whatever You Do, Don't Just Drop Out

During elections, politicians say you can't beat a somebody with a nobody. The parallel in working life is that you can't beat a rat race with nothing. By that I mean you should never drop out of a rat race into nothing. One network celebrity dropped his show, saying he was tired of all the hassle, work, and tension connected with it, and he wanted to go away and think about life. My guess is that all he needed was a month or so off. As with sex, you can get way behind in "thinking about life" and catch up in a hurry. Sometimes in just one afternoon of doing nothing you can do enough "thinking about life" to satisfy all but the most avid.

Take a month if you can and view your situation from a distance. Remind yourself that much of the hassle you experience comes from the inner tension you, yourself, create because your Critical Parent beats down on your Child, demanding perfection, hurry, etc. Learn to recognize this and turn the volume down, and at least some of the tension will disappear.

Taking Charge

You can take charge of your life, whether you're in a rat race or not, by putting your Adult ego state in control of your personality. One way to stop reacting blindly to the Critical Parent Voice within you is to start *thinking* about yourself and what you do. The robot way is to live a stimulus/response life with no *you* in between —no goals, no direction from you.

Gordon Allport, one of the most respected psychologists of our time, says: "Speaking as a psychologist and a scientist, I have to say that I think man has a great deal more freedom than he ever uses, simply because he operates out of habits, prejudices, and stereotypes, often going off, as it were, half-cocked. If he reflected and kept uppermost the selective set to ask himself, 'Is this my style of life or isn't it?' he would have a lot more self-determinism than is reflected in the traditional materialistic, mechanistic view of man as a reactive being." Dr. Allport continues that "with some nine trillion brain cells, what's going on inside the organism simply cannot be adequately depicted in terms of S-R."*

I have found that a very effective way of putting *you* between the stimulus and the response is to place your Adult in charge of a Creative Thinking session. Every three or four days, or once a week, get all by yourself and meditate. I don't mean transcendental meditation, which I think is also helpful but am not talking about here. I'm talking about a meditation period of about fifteen minutes where you actually *think*. During the meditation period you check up on yourself, away from all the stimuli that have pushed you in different directions. You tune in on your inner conversations and listen to all the "shoulds" and "oughts" that the Critical Parent is hammering at you. You place your Adult in charge and ask yourself questions like these:

- "What did I do the past few days that I enjoyed?"
- "Can I increase those enjoyment periods for myself?"
- "What did I do merely because it was expected of me?"
- "Who would I most like to approve of me? Is this a childhood feeling? Would their approval really benefit me?"
- "In what ways do I conform to custom, habit, or the wishes of others that needlessly limits my life? Which of my "shoulds" and "oughts" are nonsense?"

*Richard Evans, *Gordon Allport: The Man and His Ideas.*

- "How do I frustrate myself? Are there any ways that I work against myself, sabotage my goals?"
- "Do I still think that in order to get work done I must experience tension and strain?"
- "How much time do I spend in the here and now, versus regretting the past or worrying about the future?"
- "What mistakes have I made since the last Creative Thinking session?"
- "How can I avoid or reduce those mistakes?"
- "What are my short-term goals?"
- "What are my long-term goals in life?" If I continue as I am now doing, will I be likely to reach them? Do I sit around 'Waiting For Santa Claus' or 'Assignments From Teacher' rather than steering my own life?"
- "How do I use my premium time, those three or four hours each day when I am at my peak energy and efficiency level? Do I squander it having coffee, in minor phone calls, gossiping, dull meetings, etc.? How can I better employ my premium time to move my life along?"
- "Do I accumulate bad feelings?"
- "Do I become irritable when I come close to thinking about that which my Parent tapes say I must not examine?"
- "With my present Parent tapes, Adult knowledge, and Child feelings, can I reach my goals? If not, what do I need to change?"
- "If I were a consultant and had myself for a client, what changes would I advise?"

You can think of your own questions once you begin your Creative Thinking sessions, but the above will get you started. Take them one at a time and go slowly. These questions will help you reduce stress and improve the quality of your life, whether you are in a rat race or not. In case you're driven by an inner tyrant, don't try for "perfect" Creative Thinking sessions. They are not something you *should* do, but something you can do for yourself.

10

What It Really
Takes to Succeed

As I said in Chapter 6, several studies by major universities conclude that people get fired and miss promotions because they don't get along with others. I focused on this point in my classes by giving a questionnaire to complete. One of the questions was: "What does it take to get ahead in an organization?" The answers from undergraduates, whom another professor polled for me, were markedly different from those of graduate students I taught who were already out in the working world.

The undergraduates still have stars in their eyes. They named ingenuity, drive, long hours, creativity, hard work, in a long list of reasons why people get ahead.

Not so the graduate students who were already out in the "real" world. In class after class of older, working students, more than 90 percent said that to get ahead in an organization the most important thing is to play politics. When asked to define what they mean by "politics," they eventually come up with a class consensus that it means being a "yes" man and catering to your superiors. Or as the bluntest member of each class usually put it sooner or later, "Playing politics means you've got to kiss everybody's butt to stay a member of the in group." One student explained, "It's the small groups in organizations that are important. Often, as a man or woman moves up in an organization, he takes his own group with him. If you have ever done anything to antagonize any member of that group, God help you. You are finished as far as that organization is concerned."

The students view the prospect of playing politics as both frightening and depressing. "You've got to submerge your individuality," said one older man who had already gone far enough up the ladder to be considered a success by almost anyone's standards. "You must appear to agree, even if you are in direct opposition. You either get along or get out."

"The self-deception that people work under gets to me," one manager in his forties said during one of our seminars. His sentiments were reaffirmed by others in the class. "I've been working a long time and I have yet to find a boss who doesn't say, 'One thing I can't stand is yes men.' I'll bet I've heard that statement a hundred times, but it simply isn't true. You look at the people around the boss and they are all yes men. They put on a show of disagreeing with him on matters that don't amount to anything or that all have tacitly agreed to disagree on, but on the important issues everybody nods his head yes."

One student observed that this is human nature; we all want people around us who agree with our viewpoints. "The secret," he said, laughing, "is to put yourself in a position where a manager who thinks like you can discover you."

The students are partially right; people do like to be agreed with. But it's more complicated than the students make it. It's OK to accept authority. It's OK to agree with people. It's OK to get along in an organization. It's even OK (hold on to your tapes) to be a "yes" man, just as long as you don't have to change anything important in your life—your ideals, your religion, your husband, your wife, etc.

Almost everyone has a boss, but nobody likes authority because it means that the Child within us is not allowed to do whatever it wants to do. It puts us in the position we were in as helpless children when we had to do what we were told. It triggers our childhood feelings of Not OKness.

Some people, if they were mistreated in early life, can't stand *any* kind of authority. A word spoken to them telling them what to do triggers their Not OK, very angry Child. Others don't have such a violent reaction, but just smolder with resentment.

Some have had so much Critical Parent directed at them in their youth that they have trouble accepting it when they are older. Others, who were all but abandoned by one or both parents, had to get along with few or confusing Parent messages and, to survive, ignored all authority. These people also find it difficult to tolerate the authority of bosses in later life.

Whatever our childhood, all of us resent authority to some degree. In most cases this resentment is archaic, and it keeps us from succeeding in an organization. Winners in organizations are not the yes men and women that the students think they are, but are, rather, people who are comfortable with authority figures or who have learned how to handle their discomfort. They can say "no" without feeling hostile; they can say "yes" without feeling they are giving in or losing their integrity.

Dr. Gordon Allport said about maintaining our integrity and individuality in organizations: "Gamesmanship along with automation and bureaucratization of life tend to detract one from a personal development and leave the individual just able to get by if he joins the crowd and becomes an organization man. . . . I'm inclined [however] to think that the challenge to the healthy person is to learn to play the game where necessary, to meet the requirements of the culture, and still to have integrity; to maintain some self-objectification, and not to lose his personal values and commitments."*

How Winners Handle Authority

1. When the boss gives an order, they don't let this potentially Critical Parent message trigger their Not OK Child. Winners are not fearful of becoming yes men and women. They don't confuse

*Richard Evans, *Gordon Allport: The Man and His Ideas.*

accepting authority with compromising their integrity.

2. Winners remember their basic decision: "I'm OK—You're OK." This allows them to be comfortable with others.

3. Because many people feel Not OK, winners know they must learn to handle people who are difficult to get along with. Losers are surprised by Not OK people. They spend a lifetime searching for that nonexistent organization where everyone is easy to get along with.

4. Winners do not allow Not OK people to keep them from their goal. When the president's secretary, acting from her Critical Parent, starts giving orders as if she were the president, the loser tells her off and quits his job. The winner shrugs, complies as much as necessary, bides his time, and smiles all the way to the bank.

5. The winner knows the danger inherent in exercising authority. Losers use power to gratify their Not OK Child and then disguise their motives. This causes their downfall.

The Winning Feeling

Anyone who has ever crept out early in the morning and, in an hour's fishing, caught a big bass knows the feeling of success. But if you drive all night to get to a faraway fishing spot and then catch only one bass, you feel disappointment.

Research studies show that the feeling of success or failure does not depend on accomplishment alone; it depends on accomplishment in relation to expectations. Fulfill your expectations and you feel you've succeeded; fall short and you feel you've failed.

This dooms many to constant and pervading feelings of inadequacy because their expectations are too high. They guarantee they will feel frustration and failure because they set impossible goals. The unrealistic Child within them looks out at the world with starry-eyed anticipation and expects smooth-running days with schedules on time, promises kept, human relations pleasant, and an uninterrupted climb to the top.

In an interesting series of experiments, David McClelland of Harvard found that people with a high "need for achievement" tended to set *moderate* goals—goals that were neither extremely difficult to reach nor a cinch, but somewhere in between.*

When the inner voice of the Critical Parent is ignored, and the unrealistic expectations of the Child are brought under control, then the Adult is free to set moderate goals. Moderate goals that are within our reach allow us to achieve more because they give us the *winning feeling*. This feeling is more important than the goal itself. Once we start feeling successful, our creative energy is released.

By refusing to allow the Critical Parent to set goals that are too difficult for us to achieve, we avoid the paralyzing effect of discouragement and frustration.

Students, young and old alike, balk at the idea of setting moderate goals. They fear this will limit their lives. Nothing could be further from the truth. Setting moderate goals expands your life and increases your chances of winning.

If, for example, your Critical Parent will allow your Child to feel good about itself only if you write a best seller, or become top salesman or president of the company, the odds are great the goal will be so overwhelming that you will become discouraged and give up.

Instead, your Adult must focus on a closer objective. The Adult doesn't decide to write a book or become top salesman; it decides to write a page or make an effective call. Then, having done that successfully, it does it again.

The inner dynamics go like this: The Critical Parent tape says, "You must do something outstanding. I won't settle for less." With this demand beating down on the Child, the project becomes intolerable. The work is threatening instead of enjoyable. Finally the person gives up because he can't take the strain. The inner voice makes him feel so bad about his small accomplishments that

*D. McClelland, *The Achieving Society* (New York: D. Van Nostrand, 1961).

"What's the use?" becomes the final feeling. All productive activity stops.

The best definition I've ever heard of failure is that it's the cessation of activity. Think about this for a moment: Can you see how it is true? If you keep your goals and expectations moderate so they are possible to achieve, you'll keep trying and inch forward; but set them impossibly high, and the frustration will become so painful you'll quit entirely. . . . And *that* is failure. You see, the trick in life is to outsmart yourself.

How to Get from Here to Where You Want to Be

1. The goal should be moderate; not a cinch, but within reach. Once it is reached, a higher goal can be set. The Adult must test reality to assess the chances of reaching the goal and *determine what sacrifices* must be made to achieve it.

2. The Child ego state must be consulted for willingness to accept the sacrifices necessary to reach the goal. The Nurturing Parent must give encouragement and comfort along the way.

3. Critical Parent tapes must be turned off. Don't play:

"Who are you to try this?"
"Don't be assertive."
"Don't be hopeful."
"Don't think."
"Don't be you."
"Don't live."

4. The Adult must not allow goals to be set by the Not OK Child to gain respectability. Self-respect is a gift one bestows on oneself.

5. Keep the Child's expectations and anxiety in check. As William James advised, be "thoughtless of the outcome." Focus on the objective and the *means* to reach it and avoid what the Austrian psychiatrist Viktor Frankl calls "anticipatory anxiety."

6. Reasonable time must be allowed for the goal to be reached.

When you think you've allowed a sufficient amount of time, just to outsmart the Critical Parent, double it.

7. Once the goal is reached, enjoy it. Give yourself plenty of strokes. Allow your Child to celebrate. Nourish the feeling of success.

11

Freedom in Marriage

(Can Also Be
Applied to Dating)

With a knowledge of the application of TA, married couples can transact with each other on a more meaningful level, identify common goals, reduce misunderstandings, desensitize financial problems, decrease miserable nonproductive fighting, free their sexual relationship, experience more intimacy, and find more zest and personal freedom in living together.

When you realize that one out of three marriages ends in divorce and many others struggle on in misery, it's clear that help is desperately needed. There are many fine people in these marriages who have no idea how to find their way out of the maze they are trapped in. TA offers hope and guidelines for the journey they so eagerly started on their wedding day. At the beginning, however, I want to make clear that if you are playing hard, destructive games, you need therapy, and I hope this book hooks your Adult enough for you to seek it immediately.

For those who are not playing hard games, but are muddling

along in a "C" or even a "B-plus" marriage you'd like to improve, this chapter will show you how.

They Want to Get Married in the
Worst Way . . . and They Do

Mark and Celeste attended one of my seminars, and we came to know each other well in the course of a long day that stretched into evening. Their story is not unique; I have selected it and others in this chapter because, with minor variations, I've heard them hundreds of times. Mark and Celeste represent the thousands of couples who want to get married in the worst way . . . and do.

When Mark and Celeste embarked on marriage, only their Child ego states were involved, and even the Child needs of each partner were partially hidden. They didn't make a decision, really; they merely drifted down the stream of courtship, faster and faster, until they were swept into marriage. Their Adult and Parent ego states, essential parts of every human being, took little part in the courtship, and barely even attended the wedding. There was one brief moment before the wedding ceremony when, like lightning on a summer night, Mark's Parent flashed a "How well do you know this girl?" alarm, but Mark quickly put this out of his mind and attributed it to a lack of positive thinking. With the great times they had together, how could they possibly fail to get along? Celeste had her own brief moment of illumination when her Adult questioned abandoning her college and career plans, but the thought dissolved in the glorious expectations of a bride about to be protected and cherished forever.

Had the clergyman who joined Mark and Celeste on their wedding day been able to look into their minds, he would have seen only two Child ego states, two sets of feelings about to be united for better or for worse (or, translated into their Child expectations, "for better and better").

WEDDING DAY PICTURE

(Child Ego States Only)

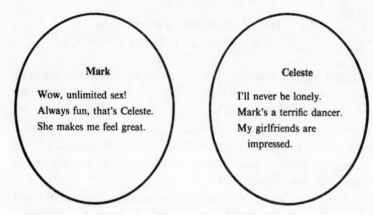

Mark

Wow, unlimited sex!
Always fun, that's Celeste.
She makes me feel great.

Celeste

I'll never be lonely.
Mark's a terrific dancer.
My girlfriends are
impressed.

Mark and Celeste Seven Years Later

As Mark and Celeste disclosed their story, it was obvious that in material ways they were luckier than the average young couple. Mark, within a year of their marriage, started a business which prospered greatly. Within several years they were able to play a superior game of Debtor,* making payments on a home in an upper-class neighborhood, two cars, including just the right foreign car, a thirty-foot cabin cruiser, and all the accouterments necessary to excel at cocktail party games of Mine Is Better Than Yours.†

The Mine Is Better Than Yours game kept Mark and Celeste frantically busy. They discovered that it takes time and effort not only to make money, but to spend it. The endless shopping, comparing, returning merchandise, talking, bargaining, checking bills, decorator conferences, delivery arrangements, entertaining, and being entertained is exhausting work. Then this proliferation of possessions requires constant maintenance and repair. The hiring and supervising of the people, only a portion of whom are trained,

*Cf. E. Berne, *Games People Play*, p. 81.
†Ibid.

to service all these things would try the patience of a saint.

Some married couples spend a lifetime playing ever-escalating versions of Mine Is Better Than Yours, with subtle differences depending on income and energy levels. Their behavior is motivated by the Child inside, which feels good only when it puts others in the shade. A Martian visiting earth to observe our culture might be astounded by the prodigious energy expended by humans as they blindly follow the unexamined idea "Get ahead of anyone you can." These couples are much like drivers who ignore the journey itself and compulsively pass every car they approach because they have never considered any other way to travel.

Mark and Celeste kept their discontent hidden from others because they played their roles so well. Nothing showed on the surface, but as each disclosed the contents of his ego states, it was obvious they were suffering human beings headed for trouble.

Mark complained of a life so intensely competitive that he rushes from one thing to another, always falling behind. He said the pressure he's under causes constant bubbling hostility just beneath the surface. He said he finds himself wondering more and more: "Is this what life is all about?" He feels like the immigrant ditchdigger who summed up his existence: "I dig the ditch to give me the money to buy the food to give me the strength to dig the ditch." Mark said, "That's my life basically. I don't even have enough energy left over for sex."

Celeste said her problem is that she is terribly bored. She doesn't feel alive. "I either roam the department stores and specialty shops looking at stuff I've seen a hundred times or I'm engaged in repetitive social events, the kind where there's a big hullabaloo about what turns out to be a small contribution to a worthy cause. I've asked Mark many times if I could get a job, but he won't consider it."

Celeste complains that Mark spends almost no time with her, and when he is at home, his mind is still at the office. Because of this inattention, her Child strikes back, not only by spending lavish amounts of money in resentment and boredom, but by letting Mark know he leaves much to be desired as a lover. This, of course, impedes Mark even more, and knowing what he faces when he gets home, he tends to stay at the office even later.

And so their story goes. Two people, luckier than most in the material world, and yet drawing further and further apart because they have no way to get in touch with themselves or with each other, driven by forces they have never examined, marching robot-like to inner voices which direct them to live a life devoid of joy or intimacy.

EGO SNAPSHOT

(Seven Years After Wedding)

Mark
Parent

Always get more and more.
A man should make more
  money every year.
Be strong.
Always hurry.

Don't show affection.

Celeste
Parent

You must be respectable.
You must be well liked.

You must be envied.
Your children must be
  perfect. (Nags.)
Your husband must be
  perfect. (Nags.)

Adult

Very shrewd in small
  matters.
Reads only financial
  material, plus
  newspapers.

Adult

Thinks very little.

Reading consists only of
  popular movie magazines.

```
          Child                        Child

  Feels OK if gets more and     Doesn't feel alive.
    more and more.
  Feels OK if ahead of others.  Craves attention, affection.
  Fearful won't make it big     Envies and resents husband,
    enough in business.           spends money to get even.
  Feels guilty about wanting    Doesn't like sex because
    to stay away from             angry with husband.
  home.
```

Fly Now and Pay Later

The wedding day ego picture of Margaret and Brian differs little from that of Mark and Celeste. Here again, mainly the Child ego states were involved, but three years later the picture in their households is different. Brian makes little money, he hates his job, and they are crushed under the weight of the debts they have incurred since they were married.

This story is told time after time to professors around the country by students who graduated in previous years and now find themselves, at a young age, with few options in life. Their job is tedious, they're deeply in debt; and now, after the Child has indulged itself to the limit, they want to throw everything over and "would sort of like to go back to school [the Child was so happy there] and get a law degree" or "I've really always wanted to be a doctor." It's a depressing story and there is no magical solution the professor can offer to people caught in what has been blithely referred to as the tender trap. It's a partial indictment of our system that we neglect to teach our young the folly of being dominated by the Child within, seeking immediate gratification.

From the day of their wedding Margaret and Brian started playing Debtor. They knew from the advertisements (and their expensive education never disputed it) that they should "Fly now and pay later" and "You only go around once" and also, "You deserve the best because you're worth it." They had no idea they were playing *roles* of carefree bride and groom, mere types in the files of motivational research organizations employed so every financial twitch of the couple could be predicted with startling accuracy.

After the honeymoon Brian and Margaret easily convinced themselves it was *necessary* to mortgage their lives to the hilt for house, cars, furniture, silverware, china, drapes, patio furniture, etc., and the culture exhorted them to play the game faster.

Then, with the finality of a prison sentence, reality moves into their mortgaged lives and holds them in an ever-tightening grip. Brian hates his job, and it hits him with crushing force that *this* is what he will be doing the rest of his life. With all their debts, Brian can't afford a week off from work, let alone time to go back to school. I've heard hundreds of couples describe their despair over the circumstances they find themselves in. "Find themselves in" is an apt expression here because they did not, in their Adult ego state, *plan* what they would do with their lives. The Child was in charge of their wedding and the creation of the huge mountain of debt. And now the bewildered inner Child blames fate for its predicament.

Conspicuous Consumption

Conspicuous consumption* is practiced by couples driven by the Critical Parent (see Chapter 2) to "be respectable," "be well liked," "be as good as 'they' are." These people are obsessed with the need to live in the right house in the right neighborhood, send their children to the right schools wearing the right clothes, belong to the right club. Their conversation is sprinkled with: "What will people think?" Their ever-increasing material wants drain their energy and resources and require constant attention. The inner

*A phrase coined by Thorstein Veblen, world-renowned American economist.

dialogue is between the Parent and the Child, with the Parent telling the Child what it must do to gain approval. The dialogue between the couple is Parent to Parent, with each telling the other the latest thing it needs to maintain respectability. In *Marital Brinkmanship,* Dr. A. H. Chapman says: "Discourse about ostentatious consumption occupies a large percentage of marital *communication.* If a demon with a tape recorder were hidden behind the sofa during a typical week in the average American home he probably would find that at least twenty percent of all conversation was directly or indirectly concerned with this aspect of life. Endless schemes, compromises and ingenious plans are made to acquire, and then maintain in satisfactory condition, all the things the rules of ostentatious waste require. Keeping this interminable gimcrackery repaired, clean and up-to-date demands constant effort. The embattled marital couple must engage in a great deal of conspiratorial work to maintain the senseless squandering on which their self-esteem and social position are based."*

A Daring Escape

Toni and Doug voluntarily became *downwardly* mobile, even though they had ample money to do what they wished. When Doug was in his thirties, and Toni ten years younger, they decided to move with their three small children from a house they owned free of any mortgage in the most expensive section of their city to a middle-class neighborhood. They told people who asked why they were moving that their youngest child had crawled over their fence and almost fallen in the river that ran by their house. But Doug confided to me this wasn't the reason at all.

He said, "You know how Toni is—she doesn't give a damn for the material gadgets or social life. I don't either; I like to be either working, reading, or doing something with Toni and the kids. But

*A. H. Chapman, *Marital Brinkmanship* (New York: G. P. Putnam, 1974), p. 209.

we got into an ungodly rat race of parties and social events, and we decided that as long as we lived in that neighborhood there was no getting out of it. So we moved to a comfortable old section of town and, to our amusement, many of our 'rich' acquaintances dropped us like a hot potato. Over all, our life style has improved greatly, we're happier, and the genuine friends we had are still our friends today."

Doug and Toni's move reminds me of a story the psychologist Abraham Maslow told at a meeting. Maslow was moved to a small town as plant manager and thought he might have to spend considerable time attending ceremonial dinners, but found his fears were unwarranted. He received no invitations at all. Maslow said this puzzled him until it dawned on him that this town was not the place for a man named Abraham. "It wasn't that they threw rocks at me," said Dr. Maslow, "but I wasn't invited. And then I realized that I carry with me, wherever I go, a semipermeable membrane. And it's wonderful because it keeps away from me all the bastards, all the stinkers; all the mean people and cruel people [prejudiced against Jews] stay away from me." The audience roared with laughter, then Maslow brought the house down when he continued: "How much would you pay for such a thing? I never did publish the idea because there was only one trouble with the semipermeable membrane. It keeps out the Gentile bastards, but it lets the bastards who are Jewish through."

Toni and Doug's move gave them a semipermeable membrane that protects them from social time-wasters who judge people by the neighborhood they live in. Today there are a number of Adult-motivated people who, as far as material things are concerned, choose to become downwardly mobile and discover that less can indeed be more. This doesn't mean they borrow an ax and build a hut by a pond, but it does mean they march to a different drummer than the one that ceaselessly beats: "Get more . . . Get more." Many know that a prevalent cause of divorce is the doctrine of spending more and more for things the couple care little about. These things are then disposed of after the divorce when both partners seek to find peace in a more simplified life.

It's well known that advertisers, agencies, and research firms spend fortunes pinpointing the exact appeal to use in advertising campaigns. If you listen closely, you can identify which Child feeling they are trying to trigger, which Parent command they are trying to activate in the buyer.

Persons Versus Things

The alternative to endless accumulation of things is not life in a commune, but life governed by the Adult, with freedom to select that which increases the quality of life instead of the quantity of trappings. The Adult protects the Child from Parental commands such as: "You must be top dog." "You must make me proud of you." "You must outdo the Joneses." Couples who manage their finances from their Adult discover options in their life they didn't know they had. They escape the anxiety that accompanies conspicuous consumption. Since conflict over money is cited as one of the biggest problems in marriage, they greatly increase their chances for a happy marriage. They also find that people can be persons with one another and not mere symbols of economic or career success. There *are* people, perhaps not many, who are free to experience *human relations* in the deepest meaning of the words. They relate, in Martin Buber's words, in an "I-Thou" encounter and not "I-It."

Observe the hustling I-It couple of today and listen to their involved exchange of information on their standing in the what-do-you-own or who-do-you-know hierarchy. By innuendo and allusion they artfully, or not so artfully, contrive to win at Mine Is Better Than Yours. One such woman could have gone all the way to the finals for the most status symbols dropped in the fewest words when she said: "I was fearful my daughter would catch cold in our pool after her strenuous tennis lesson and be unable to enter her horse in the show; but luckily, our downstairs maid had thought to turn on the pool heater—she's been the savior of our family for twenty years." That lady would have been outclassed, though, by the vulgarity of the couple whose Christmas card consisted of a montage of their most expensive property, including a waterfront mansion, a palatial summer home, a sixty-foot yacht, and a twin-engine airplane. One of the guests at their Christmas party remarked to them that what they really needed now was their own aircraft carrier. He was never invited back.

Intimate Communication In Marriage

A goal to strive for in marriage is what I call "I feel" communication. This goal is predicated on the fact that the Child within each of us, no matter what our age, is a very important part of our personality; yet the needs and wishes of the Child are often ignored and hidden from the marriage partner. This secretiveness is understandable when we remember that in our childhood many of us were not allowed to show our feelings. We were not allowed to take pleasure in our bodies. If we showed anger, displeasure, or resentment, we were often punished. Curiosity about sex was discouraged, and in some families, even affection was turned away. Anything connected with sexuality was given such exaggerated importance that nothing straight dared be said at all. Whole generations of children are raised to believe that you must come on crooked about sex. (See Chapter 12, Raising OK Children.) Grown men and women gather around the TV set to watch Leer and Laugh shows, in which the M.C., with a leer and obviously in his Child ego state, refers to sex obliquely and then everybody is so charged up they roar with laughter.

The Child inside cries out for attention, affection, recognition, and nurturing. But as we grow older, the Child learns it must get all these things in crooked ways or the inner Parent will raise hell. So the Child stays hidden and connives to gratify its needs. What a sad paradox that in marriage we have these deep and powerful desires, yet keep them hidden for a lifetime from those we love.

In "I Feel" communication, the couple practices disclosing the *feelings* of their Child rather than attacking with the same old Parent tapes. The husband who does not want his wife to work does not attack her position with memorized tapes: "You'll stay home because I say so." "The woman's place is in the home." "I'm old-fashioned and not ashamed of it." Instead, he tells his wife where he is in the here and now by saying: "Your leaving the home makes me feel very threatened." "I feel abandoned with you out of the house." "I'm afraid you would find someone you'd like better." "I feel I would lose control over you." "I feel" statements don't automatically solve the problem, but they open the way to mutual agreement. The old memorized statements, dissembling, and outright attacks always aggravate the problem. Other examples of "I feel" statements in marriage are:

Spouse No. 1	Spouse No. 2
I feel terrible about missing that promotion.	I understand how you feel. Let's talk about it.
When you're reluctant to make love, I feel unwanted, clumsy, and undesirable.	I didn't know it made you feel that way. Let me tell you why I'm hesitant. It's not what you believe at all.
When you interrupt me I feel like breaking up the furniture.	It's a bad habit of mine. Tell me why you feel so angry about it.
I feel lonely and unnecessary now that N. has gone away to college.	I feel bad too, but you're necessary to me. Let's go out and have some fun together.
I felt inferior to S. at the party tonight.	Do you know what triggered your Not OK feeling?
I feel so hurt and resentful when you say that.	I'm sorry. It was my Critical Parent taking over. It's not what I really mean.

The Karpman* C.A.S.E. System

Several months after the final manuscript for this book went to the publisher, I talked with Stephen B. Karpman, M.D., psychiatrist and creator of many ideas in Transactional Analysis that give helpful insights. Dr. Karpman worked with Dr. Eric Berne to discover why both single and married people did not experience more meaningful and satisfying relationships. As we talked, it was clear that Dr. Karpman is convinced, and I agree with him, that many couples can't talk through their problems; they are unable to state in clear language *what they want.* "If they would learn to search their inner selves," says Dr. Karpman, "recognize what it is they want, and then state their wants, many of their problems would be solved." The goal here is intimacy in communication.

Dr. Karpman has identified the following blocks to intimate communication and makes them easy to remember by the acronym, C.A.S.E. Say that a person has something important that he wants to talk to his partner about, the partner blocking communication then becomes:

*C*ondescending. The condescending partner takes the attitude there is something wrong with the other, with what he says or how he brings it up—as if the other person would not know how to solve the problem, or as if what he says will make no difference anyway. The condescending partner takes the other's gold and turns it into straw.

*A*brupt. The partner blocks intimacy by sudden disengagement: slamming doors; leaving the room; saying, "I don't want to talk about it;" etc. The abrupt partner is intimidating.

*S*ecretive. The partner blocks intimacy by keeping information, good strokes, or good feelings hidden that would be of benefit in solving the problems of the relationship.

*E*vasive. The evasive partner blocks intimacy by confusing the

*Permission granted by Stephen B. Karpman, M.D., Transactional Analysis Spring Conference, Atlanta, Georgia.

issue, getting the other off the track, avoiding the subject. Sometimes the point is forgotten, or it's felt not worth the effort to get back to it.

For behavior that achieves intimacy between couples, where the partners talk about the things that are important to them and give each other a print-out on their inner selves, Dr. Karpman has identified a better C.A.S.E. In this C.A.S.E., the partners are:

*C*herishing. The partners let each other know by words, gestures, tones and touch that they treasure each other, that they hold each other in high regard, that their relationship is very important to them. Cherishing partners make each other look good. No matter what a partner may say, there will be at least ten per cent the other can agree with, ten per cent that is truth. The cherishing partner will find that ten per cent and build from there.

*A*pproachable. This is primarily a non-verbal attitude. The partners are accepting and open, and, by their welcoming manner, they invite each other to say what they want to say.

*S*urrendering. The partners give up their "secret dossiers" and disclose their inner thoughts and feelings. They drop their masks, tell that which is difficult to tell, and give each other a chance to explain, enlighten and defend.

*E*ngaged. The partners stay with the subject long enough to work it through. They are patient, occupied and involved with each other.

I'd like to add that Dr. Karpman practices what he preaches. He is a warm, trusting, open human being who has devoted his life to helping the harried human race and who, himself, communicates in a meaningful and intimate way.

Be Manly—Don't Show Emotion

George was raised in a harsh, prickly environment where affection was neither given nor received. He was taught that crying, showing disappointment, expressing fears, displaying love and affection were not "manly." He remembers that whenever as a child he tried to hug or kiss his mother, she would brush him off with: "Go on now." "Don't be silly. That's for sissies." "Don't bother me." With both words and disapproving looks, George's mother implanted in George's mind the message: "Don't get close." As a result, George grew up feeling there was something wrong about people being close to each other or showing their emotions in any way. George's stern father demonstrated the way to keep people at a distance.

Now, years later, Ann sits across the room from George and quietly fumes. They have been married for several years and George seems to withdraw more and more into himself with each passing year. Ann noticed when they were dating that George showed little affection and never spoke words of endearment. She found the "strong, silent" treatment rather romantic during court-ship because it surrounded George with mystery. But now that she suspects that George will be detached and withdrawn the rest of their lives, she is not sure she can stand it. Ann has a Child within that demands affection in order to feel OK. She needs nurturing, but the strokes she gets from George are as infrequent as rain in the desert.

How to Communicate Child Feelings

It's difficult, when your Child inside feels bad, to tell someone —no matter how much you love the person—how you feel. Here are a few points to remember for those who want to practice disclosing their feelings to each other in a straightforward way:

1. The partner should strive to listen with unconditional accept-ance. The Child is accustomed to hiding its real feelings, especially Not OK feelings. At the slightest sign of disapproval, it will be back to its old tricks of coming on crooked. It's helpful to think of yourself as a professional therapist. You can be certain a psycholo-gist or psychiatrist wouldn't say to a patient, "My God, you surely can't be serious. You must be crazy."

2. Don't intellectualize your feelings. You can avoid this by beginning your statements, "I feel . . ." This is not the time for philosophy and abstractions. Your partner is making it safe for you to tell how you really feel.

3. Try to identify your basic feeling. Often fear disguises itself as anger. Maybe you are angry with your partner for flirting with Sally at the party, but the more basic feeling is that you're fearful he finds Sally more attractive.

4. Try to *be* what you are feeling. This is what some psychologists term "congruence." Your outward appearance should be congruent with your inner feeling. The most common example of a person who is not being congruent is one who, with face grimly set, says through clenched teeth, "No, I'm not angry. I'm not angry at all. What makes you think that?"

5. Confirm what your partner has been trying to convey with such phrases as: "Do you mean you feel this way?"

6. Nurture each other as much as possible during these encounters. Intimacy is very difficult for most people in our society. Sometimes what one partner may reveal is hurtful to the other. It may even start an argument, but an argument about genuine feelings is usually better than silent resentment. Mutual supportiveness and nurturing will minimize hurt feelings and will bring the couple closer together.

Parental Prohibitions and Injunctions in Marriage

At a workshop I conducted in New Orleans, one man, later, over coffee, came up with an interesting idea. We had been talking about the "Don't succeed" command, and he said he suddenly realized that he was struggling against a "Don't succeed" command not only in his career but also in his marriage. He said he could remember his mother telling him as a young child he was just like his father and would never amount to anything. "My father left us when I was less than a year old," he said, "and it made her bitter against men the rest of her life. Her messages to me were always

ones of defeat and discouragement. Gloom pervaded our home.
Now she seems intent on sabotaging my marriage. She accuses my
wife of saying things she didn't say. She plays a victim role con-
stantly. She suffers imaginary slights from all of us, including my
six-year-old daughter. She makes* everyone feel guilty without
their knowing why. But what I really fear," he continued, "are the
terrible dark moods that sweep over me. When I'm in these moods
I want to destroy my career, marriage, and everything I've accomplished. Everything seems hopeless. I feel there's no use in trying."

I asked him if he knew why he felt this way. He replied, "I
believe it's the old Child feelings in me taking over, trying to fulfill
the prophecy of Mom that I couldn't succeed no matter how hard
I tried. The feeling has the force of a curse, and since my Child
didn't know any better at the time she was telling me these things,
it had no way to fight back." He smiled at this point and added,
"But you know, those ideas of Eric Berne's as you presented them
today about the Adult taking charge of the personality have given
me a new way to think about myself. I've made a decision that I
will continue to succeed in both my career and my marriage. My
Adult can take care of my Child, and I can ignore that inner voice
telling me, 'You're no damned good. You will never succeed at
anything.' "

Not everyone can sense the forces at war within himself as
quickly as this intelligent man did. He realizes that his Adult
decision that it's OK to succeed and OK to succeed in marriage
is much more easily said than done. The Parent voice will strike
back, and it will add to its repertoire: "Psychology is nonsense. TA
is a fad. Don't think about yourself." If it seems far-fetched that
a person could have an inner command "Don't succeed," just stop
and think of the people you know or have read about, husbands
and wives, career men and women, politicians, who have, with

---

*See "Your Defense Against Negative Strokes" in Chapter 5. She doesn't
"make" everyone feel bad; she *invites* them to feel bad. They can choose to decline
her invitation.

self-destructive sureness, sabotaged their own marriage or reputation for no apparent reason. How many times have you heard: "I have no idea why I did that."

Critical Parent Mother to Critical Parent Wife

Jeff believed he had found a girl who was the opposite of his mother. His mother criticized his every move, both as a child and even now as a man. She operated full-time, 50,000-watt Critical Parent. There was absolutely nothing anyone could do to please her. Her four marriages and one unhappy child were proof of this. Jeff always felt bad inside because his Child had tried hard to please the one person he depended on for life, his mother, for many years and had failed.

Had Jeff not been lucky enough to have had very supportive grandparents, he very possibly could have ended up in prison. As it was, he directed his Not OK feeling into socially accepted aggression and became a very successful businessman; but his "Type A" behavior (see "Tension, Worry, and Conditional Living in Chapter 4") may earn him an early grave because he drives himself without mercy, still trying to earn the approval of the Critical inner voice that nags on and on.

When Jeff married Rose, he thought she was everything a man could desire. She was all sweetness and light. She looked at him with adoring eyes and treated his every utterance as gospel. What a difference from Mom!

Rose played a role during courtship (not an unprecedented occurrence). She sensed that Jeff's Child could not stand criticism and needed constant approval. She was willing to do this when nothing more was at stake than deciding what restaurant or movie to go to. On the big issues, when Jeff was expansive, Rose found no difficulty in agreeing with him about the appropriate size of the defense budget or aid to Iran.

Now that they're married, Rose criticizes Jeff freely. This throws

Jeff into panic. His Child feels as if it's back under the same old domination by his mother. He can't accept reimprisonment. He must escape, and escape he does—into sixteen-hour working days, which proves the old adage that many a man owes his success to his mother (or wife).

How to Turn Off Tapes That Sabotage Your Marriage

Broadcasters know that if you wish to use a recording tape again, you can erase the tape completely with a magnetic bulk eraser. Presto. You've got a fresh start. You're all set to put completely new material on the tape with no distortion or feedback from the old material. We should have such a machine to erase the Critical tapes in marriage. These tapes that control our lives, that invite us to feel bad about ourselves, that play on and on with no cerebration involved, are responsible for most of today's divorces. If we can't erase these tapes, we can learn to ignore them. Here are some of the most frequently mentioned destructive tapes in marriage:

"Don't enjoy yourself."
"Don't enjoy sex."
"Don't show emotion."
"Don't be you."
"Don't give strokes."
"Don't trust strokes."
"Don't get close."
"Don't ever relax."
"Don't live in the present.
"Don't discuss anything that leads to disagreement."
"Don't disclose your feelings."
"Don't succeed."

If the injunctions in the mind are the right combination, and they often are, the couple will not be able to communicate with each other on a meaningful level. If the "Don't think" injunction exists in one or both partners, they are blocked from analyzing their problem. Add to these injunctions the following rigid "how to" messages and you can see why many marriages are in extreme difficulty:

1. How to be a good wife/husband. (This totally separate from what spouse wants—e.g., keep a spotless house, work day and night.)

2. How to make love. (Lights off, under the covers, etc.)

3. How to celebrate birthdays. (Expensive presents, trips, parties.)

4. How to celebrate Mother's Day. (Much ritual, little emotion.)

5. How to suffer a loss. (Get drunk, depressed, angry.)

6. How to spend money. (Always spend more than you can afford.)

7. How to be respectable. (Right house, car, clothes, schools, etc.)

8. How to be successful. (Work until you bring on a heart attack.)

9. How to be liked. (Agree to all demands, serve on all committees.)

10. How to raise children. (Military obedience.)

To liberate themselves from these Critical and controlling tapes, husbands and wives must give themselves *permission* from their Adult to listen to these injunctions and "how to"s so they will be aware of what is driving them on. They must then give themselves permission to examine these inner messages. Each can be a therapeutic agent to the other through Creative Listening (see Chapter 7), setting a climate in which each is free to be transparent. They can disclose Parent tapes and Child feelings to each other for the partner to handle with loving care and in this way give meaning, depth, and hope to their marriage. Finally, each can make a *decision* in his Adult to ignore the archaic Critical voices that cause so much trouble. The married couple can give themselves permission to enjoy one another, their marriage, their children, and their life.

Don't be discouraged when you find the Critical voices difficult to override. They're a force to be reckoned with. Once you give yourself permission to ignore them, they may return to torment you until they are finally conquered by the Adult. Say, for example, the Parent tape in your head commands, "Don't enjoy sex," and is combined with strict "how to" rules. You and your spouse discuss this and, in your Adult, give yourselves powerful permission to enjoy closeness and sex. The Parent voice in your head may berate you, cast doubt on your character, trigger your Not OK Child feelings, and raise all kinds of hell to get you back in line. Don't be surprised; don't give up. Remember that you made an Adult decision to enrich your marriage, keep it off the rocks and out of the divorce court, and to get more joy from life. Fight back with all you've got. Decide whether you prefer to have the good will of the Critical Parent or a good marriage and a contented spouse. If necessary, to strengthen your Adult, write down the reasons you decided in favor of your Adult reasoning and OK Child feelings. Review this decision whenever the inner tyrant strikes. Remember, you're only a decision away from freedom. You decide to operate in your Adult and give your suffering inner Child (and your partner's) a break.

What the Adult Should Know About Marriage

Many people have opinions about marriage recorded in their Parent ego state that are simply not true. This accumulated lore and legend accounts for much of the present trouble in marriage. Let's examine some of the facts the Adult should know about marriage. If you find yourself disagreeing, note your objection as it flashes through your mind, then review your thinking to see whether you have an unsuspected Parent tape on the subject, or if perhaps your Parent or Child has contaminated what your Adult should know.

1. The Adult knows there are no norms for happiness in marriage. Some couples make themselves miserable because they think

it's normal to be happy all the time. Happiness for everyone, single or married, is episodic. It comes and goes, and sometimes for no apparent reason.

2. The Adult knows, by the same reasoning, there are no norms for sexual fulfillment in marriage. Sex cannot be calibrated like a height and weight chart so you'll know how many times a week is normal at what age. It varies for each couple, and within a marriage it varies depending on what is going on in the couple's life. The sex goddesses on the movie and television screens, with their baby talk and breathless panting calculated to imply they have to tear themselves away from the bedroom, are in many cases frigid women. They have had multiple marriages, not because the beast within them cannot be satisfied, but contrarily, because they know neither how to give nor how to receive love.

In the absence of reliable statistics, you can only say that sexual activity depends on the wants and needs of each partner in the marriage, and people are as different here as in every other aspect of life. It is important that whatever these wants and needs are, they be satisfied in the marriage. There is only one way to discover the real needs of the partner and that is to discuss them in an open and acceptant climate, free of all the ridiculous injunctions and taboos placed on this important subject. If our society had placed such taboos on eating, it might well be that a married partner would find it necessary to sneak out at night for a rare roast beef sandwich, or blush, stammer, and finally get very angry when his spouse brought up the subject of serving lamb chops. Sexual taboos, the unwillingness to discuss them, the refusal to meet the partner's needs and wants, the insisting that sexual tension can be relieved only by intercourse, the use of sex as a weapon—all are just as ridiculous. If you have a large collection of sexual taboos in your Parent and sexual feelings in your Child, they may be difficult to communicate, but not nearly as difficult as the searing meanness of a divorce or silent suffering over the years.

An experiment conducted at a major university showed that couples who were happy had sex twice a week. (There, your Child knew there was a norm for sexual happiness, didn't it? And now you feel good because you're above the average or bad because you're below it. Well, read on.) The researchers also found that those couples who were *unhappy* had sex twice a week. The difference between the two couples was that in the unhappy couples, both the husband and wife reported that twice a week suited them fine, but the unhappy wives thought it was less sex than the husband wanted, and the unhappy husbands thought it was more sex than the wife wanted. Both the unhappy and the happy couples had the same amount of sex, but the unhappy couples, although each was satisfied with their sex activity, thought the other wasn't. They thought their problem was sex, but it was communication.

3. The Adult knows that one half plus one half does not equal a whole in marriage. A person with strong Not OK feelings in his inner Child does not suddenly become OK in marriage. A neurotic need is sometimes mistaken for love, but marriage itself cannot make up for the deficiency in one or both partners. An inner Child that becomes flooded with feelings of anger, depression, guilt, resentment, inadequacy, will continue to experience these feelings in marriage.

4. The Adult knows that having children is not the answer for a shaky marriage. There's a popular notion that children cement a marriage together. It's true that children can be a joy and a blessing in a marriage that is already stable, but children require sacrifice. They may become innocent victims in a marriage that can't handle the stress.

5. The Adult knows that his Child feelings about his spouse and about the institution of marriage will fluctuate. He knows there will be good days and bad days, and he does not allow himself to take the bad days too seriously.

6. The Adult creates an atmosphere in which his partner's Child can tell its feelings in safety. The Adult listens and allows its Parent to nurture and protect when desirable. The Adult can decide when the situation is serious enough to require professional help.

7. The Adult knows that critical statements can destroy any human relationship. If he has too many critical Parent tapes and too few Nurturing Parent tapes from his own childhood, he can re-Parent himself by ignoring the Critical tapes and replacing them with Nurturing tapes. Married couples help one another survive and grow by treasuring each other.

8. The Adult tries to come on straight in expressing the needs and wants of his Child. He respects the needs and desires of his partner and looks for a solution that satisfies both. He does not view this as an I-win-you-lose proposition, but as I-win-you-win. He knows that time can be restructured away from destructive games such as Uproar, See What You've Made Me Do, If It Weren't For You, Frigid Man, Frigid Woman.*

9. Some psychologists recommend that all marital fighting be kept constructive. This can happen when the Adult ego states are involved in the disagreement, but a fight, even in the best of marriages, is sometimes going to get mean when the Child ego states go at it. It's best when this happens that you don't berate yourself for not being as civilized as other couples. I suspect that some marriages appear civilized because the partners have stopped caring about each other enough to even bother to fight. The opposite of love is not the hate that the Child of a spouse may show in a marital spat, but indifference. Remember that your spouse may be a giant of a person and yet have torments hidden in his Child that must be worked through. In a marital fight the Child may storm around making terrible remarks. Many couples admit, ashamedly, to this. The best thing is to not take it all that seriously. Picture what's really happening as a fight between two five-year-olds. Sure, try to keep the fight constructive, but if it isn't and becomes a character assassination, it is very important that you and your spouse forgive and forget. You can't hold a grudge against a Child for long, can you?

*Cf. E. Berne, *Games People Play.*

10. The Adult strives to keep damage to a minimum. During an argument, it tries to hook the Adult of the partner. Failing this, it shortens the fight and, most important of all, does not let the Child of either feel guilty because their attempt at a better marriage broke down. The adult knows there are bound to be setbacks. Couples in their Adult know that love *does* mean saying you're sorry. They know the hurt, Not OK Child says terrible things it doesn't mean.

11. The Adult knows the Child in both partners must have some fun. They remember the carefree days of courtship and, in creative ways that have meaning for them, they return to those days and enjoy each other. This is not only psychologically imperative, but also practical because in recreating themselves, they give their Adults much better problem-solving ability.

12. The Adult sets *specific* behavioral objectives to improve his marriage. Contracting to "improve" is too broad to be operational. The husband and wife should make clearly defined contracts with each other to, for example, give each other a compliment every morning, never criticize each other in front of anyone, practice Creative Listening, discuss each other's Parent tapes, etc. They might also contract to give up destructive teasing and discounting. Teasing is often the Not OK Child's game of one-upmanship, putting the other person one down, but laughing all the while to avoid retaliation. (Nobody wants to be a poor sport.)

13. The Adult knows there are no magic solutions. There are no books, courses, or counselors that can change the couple unless they make an Adult *decision* to change. They can either continue their harmful patterns as if they played no part in them, but are merely innocent bystanders at their own destruction, or they can, as Shakespeare said, "take arms against a sea of troubles and by opposing, end them." The decision is theirs and theirs alone. Once they decide, they may not need help, but if they do need help, they should by all means seek it.

12

Raising OK Children

(Can Also Be Applied
to Your Own Inner Child)

Many men and women make themselves miserable trying to be perfect parents. They go to bed at night feeling guilty or vaguely uneasy because they have not reached a standard of parenthood they think desirable, but which, in reality, is achieved by no one. They become parent-training junkies, anxiously studying the latest theory, trying the newest technique, only to be tripped up for the thousandth time when Junior glares at them with defiance, daughter refuses to answer questions about the party, or number-one son clouts number-two son and makes him cry.

After talking with hundreds of parents after classes and speeches, I'm convinced that many men and women find parenthood an experience which leaves them feeling drained and dissatisfied. And they don't know what to do about it. They want the relationship to be peaceful and loving, they want their children to find happiness and fulfillment, they want them to be "straight" and not lead bent and crooked lives, but they have little information to guide them other than dialogues written by "experts" where *one*

151

parent faces *one* child at a time, with nothing on the parent's mind but effective human relations (never mind dinner, taxes, inflation, sickness, possible job loss, rushing to the airport, meetings, guests arriving, housework, exhaustion, etc.), and with perfect control, calmly states his truth; and the child answers, "Gosh, Mom/Dad, I never thought of it that way."

Communication is important, and we'll explore better ways to communicate with our children and solve the problems parents and children living under the same roof encounter. But before we do, the parent who wants to find more joy and less stress in raising his children must make two admissions and *remember* them. Your Parent voice may raise hell with these admissions, your inner Child may feel guilty, but I can assure you they are true, and in your Adult you'll know it.

1. You can never be a perfect parent. You are bound to make mistakes, lose control, shout, storm, fight, cuff, punish, berate, sulk, or stew, because you are human. Parents are not perfect people, so they will not be perfect parents.

2. You are not omnipotent. You are the most important influence in the life of your child, but how he'll turn out depends also on other factors, including: your spouse, inherited traits, intelligence level, teachers, schools, friends at school and at home, opportunities, economic developments, political developments.

So relax, take a deep breath, loosen the muscles at the back of your neck, and repeat: "Parents are not perfect" and "Parents are not omnipotent." If you want to be an effective parent, you must accept yourself and your children as the imperfect creatures we all are. Decide to be a B-plus parent. The only one who ever comes close to straight A's in raising children is the expert writing calm, reasonable advice in a secluded room: The child does X, and Mother, instead of selecting response Y, decides on response Z, and sweet reason prevails.

Unfortunately, events in families do not happen one at a time. That's not life. The measured, thoughtful response is not always possible when life is pushing hard and fast. I read a magazine interview some time ago that haunts me still. The wife of a prisoner of war told the interviewer that people tend to think that the torment of having a husband in prison camp is the *only* problem you have. They forget that life keeps coming at you. The car still breaks down, the children get sick and get into scrapes at school, you need an operation, bills have to be paid. Problems sometimes crowd us and we find precious little time to practice perfect child psychology. One child expert on a television talk show became visibly upset when asked if he had any children of his own. He testily replied, "That has nothing to do with anything. You can analyze a parade better sitting on the curb than marching in it." I don't agree with him. The emotions in any experience are the heart of it. You can't give advice on marching in a parade without knowing from experience how tired you can get.

The Old Parental Self-Torture Game

Dinner is nearly ready, two of the children are bickering loudly, and Mom is tired but grimly determined not to get angry. It's hot in the kitchen, the argument grows louder, and someone drops a jar of honey, which breaks into fifty sharp sticky pieces on the kitchen floor. At that moment, a third child happens in and cuts his foot on the broken glass. The stew boils over and so does Mom. She blows her stack, makes a few hasty accusations and a couple of character defamations. The two who were arguing are sent to bed hungry. After an uneasy evening, Mom looks in on the two peacefully sleeping "criminals," and vows never to get that angry with them again. She tosses and turns much of the night. The next day, after they have been home from school not more than ten minutes, Mom's solemn vow is broken again, and she is left with the familiar feeling of failure and frustration.

The goal of a B-plus parent is to be a good parent—not perfect, just good—making mistakes, losing control, getting back on the track as quickly as possible, apologizing, and throwing in large measures of self-forgiveness. The B-plus parent stops the self-torture game because he knows it's OK to blow his top once in a while, and there is no way he, or anyone else, can avoid it. He stops torturing himself for falling short of an idealized image of what a parent should be, an ideal that no one can attain.

Permissions for the Child

Realistic parents who have decided to ignore the "You must be perfect" tape give themselves permission to relax, enjoy, and just do the best they can. Once they let go of the rigid requirements they have placed on themselves and their children, they can think about their child's *real* needs, not what the taped messages in their head say he needs. They will find the child needs some very special permissions. As you read this Chapter, whether you have children or not, think back to your own childhood. You may decide you need to give *yourself* some of the following permissions.

Permission to Think

Some parents are so busy being Superparent that they make almost all the child's decisions for him. They forget that one of the best legacies a parent can give his child is the freedom to think for himself and make his own wise decisions as he enters the world. Kahlil Gibran expressed this idea beautifully in *The Prophet.* He was speaking about children in the following excerpt:

> They come through you but not from you,
> And though they are with you yet they belong not to you.
> You may give them your love but not your thoughts,
> For they have their own thoughts.
> You may house their bodies but not their souls,
> For their souls dwell in the house of tomorrow,
> Which you cannot visit, not even in your dreams.*

*K. Gibran, *The Prophet* (New York: Alfred A. Knopf, 1958), p. 17.

Gretchen is an extreme example of a parent who decides almost everything for her child. From the time he was very young, she has told him what clothes to wear, whom to play with, what to play, where to go, what to eat, what books to read. At first the boy tried to use his own mind, but after being told he was wrong time after time, he learned it was safer to ask Mother. That way he avoided feeling bad, and he later decided Mother knew best anyway.

Gretchen gave other "Don't think" messages. (See Chapter 8: A New Way to Solve Problems.) When the boy asked questions, Gretchen squelched him with: "I'm too busy now." "Don't bother your head about that." "You shouldn't ask such questions." "You let me worry about that." As the boy grew older, Gretchen continued making his decisions. She decided in favor of Boy Scouts and against Little League. She opted for the school band and settled on a trumpet for the instrument. The boy's few friends went to a public high school, but Mother decided on a private school that would "really require him to think."

Whenever the boy showed any spark of thinking for himself, she reminded him of a mistake he had committed years earlier when he made a decision of his own. The boy remembers the mistake keenly and is afraid of making another one. He knows this won't happen if he lets Mother do his thinking for him.

In addition to making his decisions, Gretchen further "helps" the boy by implanting a complete set of ready-made instructions in his mind. A few of the subjects covered are:

How to please important people.
How to keep very busy.
How to choose the "right" friends.
How to be a nice boy.
How to make meaningless conversation.
How to do things well that don't even need doing.
How to tell convenient lies.
How to avoid intimacy with anyone at any time.

Gretchen is guilty of smother love. As a result, whenever her boy is confronted with a question, his brain fogs over. He responds to any call for cerebration with: "Gee, I don't know." Problems cause his mind to draw a blank because he has never solved any on his own.

The "Don't think" injunction may be compounded in school. The elementary school teacher is sometimes honed in on how the children should sit in their seats, the crossing of t's, memorization and the quick regurgitation of answers. Students in this kind of classroom atmosphere don't dare hesitate, question premises, or explore alternatives. As one educator put it, "Much of our education today consists of material going from the notebook of the teacher to the notebook of the student without passing through the head of either." The "Don't think" injunction is so pervasive in our culture that it needs further explanation. Because of early conditioning, many people spend their lives, just as they did in school, in a pastime I call "Waiting for Assignments from Teacher." The little Child within the grown person lets life pass him by as he quietly waits for further instructions. He doesn't know he could run his own life, find his own answers. Irwin Edman, who was a professor at Columbia University, said in, "First Lesson": "They come to this class hoping to find out by the end of the year what it is that they are studying. And, as I am a disciple of Socrates, I do not propose to tell them. I propose, by asking the proper questions, to have them tell me, and to assist them in the discovery that they have in essence always known what philosophy is." He continues: "If only one can get them to be critical of their most usual preconceptions, one is on the road. . . . These students are very young, but they are already full of age-old prejudices."*

How many times have you heard someone say, "I feel confused"? But confusion is a state of mind, not a feeling. The person who says he feels confused means that he has been presented with a problem that short-circuits his mind. If his brainpower has been used mainly to memorize the exports of Venezuela, he will have little tolerance for ambiguity. He may require immediate closure.

*I. Edman, *Philosopher's Quest*, (New York: Viking Press, 1974).

Children learn to think in an atmosphere where thinking is encouraged. They think when it is safe to think. In a true learning environment you hear statements like the following:

"Let me know what you decide."

"I like your idea; do you see any disadvantages to it?"

"I trust you to come up with the right solution."

"That's one answer; are there any others?"

"So you made a mistake. What did you learn from it?"

"How do you know he's an expert? Do experts ever disagree?"

The parent or teacher who insists that no mistakes be made misses the essence of learning. Mistakes have high information value. As professional basketball players learn by shooting and adjusting, shooting and adjusting, so must the child be taught that the way to grow and survive in his environment is by experimenting and adjusting. The experimentation, error, and adjustment *is* learning. The child must be taught to enter the problem and look around, take his time, seek further information. Fast, memorized answers sometimes preclude the child's seeing the whole truth. Once he has been told the answer is "gravity" or "instinct" or "the healing process," he may be misled into believing he understands what is essentially a mystery to the finite human mind. In Goethe's *Faust,* Mephistopheles says, "There's always a pompous word to serve for what we may or may not understand." Part of the fault lies with our language. Some languages make allowance for man's fundamental ignorance by saying, "We *call* that gravity." The child who has been given permission to think can reason beyond mere words and perceive his world more accurately.

Permission to Think Versus Obedience

A child under a "Don't think" injunction is definitely more obedient than a child with permission to think. It's much easier on the parents. Barney and June's children never ask "Why?" They know the answer is: "Because I say so." They always say, "Yes, sir" and "No, ma'am," and they never interrupt. They are a marvel to other parents.

June and Barney met and married when they were both in the Marines during the Korean War. Together they have built a successful insurance business through discipline and hard work. They are very well organized, but they have carried it too far. They don't allow their own Natural Child any fun, and they don't permit enough free time for play and relaxation for their children. They are not unkind people. They love their children, but they think they should be raised much the same way the Marine Corps turns raw recruits into hardened soldiers. They have the idea that the way to prepare their children for a cruel world is by being a little mean with them as they're growing up. They think that discipline is an end in itself instead of a characteristic to be developed in their children so they can use it to achieve important goals in their lives. Barney and June need to develop the thinking, problem-solving Adult in their children. They exercise too much discipline and impoverish the Adult and Child ego states of their children.

But children do need guidelines that set the limits of safe activity for them. G. K. Chesterton describes a scene in which some children live on a high promontory jutting over the sea. They are safe and secure, frolicking within the walls that run around the edge of the cliff until someone, wishing to set them free, tears down the walls. Without a known safe boundary, the children are last seen huddled fearfully together.*

We don't have to choose between having a disciplined or a thinking child. The goals are not conflicting, but complementary. The best way to discipline a child, in most cases, is by strengthening his Adult. ("Son, you broke that window; it will cost money to replace. You plan how to pay me back for it.") And very often, the best way to strengthen his Adult is through discipline. ("You say

*G. K. Chesterton, *Orthodoxy* (New York: Dodd, Mead, 1936); Image Books, p. 145.

your bicycle is getting old and you'd like a new one? Figure how much you can save from your allowance and odd jobs. When you have saved up half, I'll pay for the other half.")

The most effective discipline is appropriate and consistent. The Adult in the child cannot compute contradictory messages like the following: "If you hit your little brother again, I'm going to beat the daylights out of you" (Absurd Lesson No. 1 on nonviolence). "I'll teach you not to swear around this house, you blankety-blank little S.O.B." (Absurd Lesson No. 2 on purity of speech).

Permission to Give and Receive Love

The child must have permission to give and receive love. The giving of love takes many forms. The father and mother give love to the child merely by going to work and maintaining a home. But no child, any more than an adult, can live by bread alone. His spirit is not nourished just because he is eating every day and has a room indoors. He must receive love in other manifestations.

A clergyman I met at a seminar in Ohio told about taking his son to the airport. It was the boy's first time away from home, and he was leaving his family for college. "As he walked down the ramp away from me, my heart cried out to him," said the minister, " 'Oh, my son, why didn't I, every single day, let you know how very much I love you.' "

You and I should not delay giving love to our children as a daily gift, even many times daily. It can take many forms—a welcome-home hug, a "well done" on a report card, Creative Listening to a problem, accepting an apology, giving the benefit of the doubt, saying thank you. And giving love certainly includes saying straight and sincerely, "Son [Daughter], I love you very much." This is very difficult for some parents. They want to say, "I love you," but say, instead, "Don't catch cold," which the child interprets as nagging. Expressing our love may seem awkward at first, but with practice it's easy.

In giving love and strokes, the parent teaches the child to give strokes in return and, at the same time, places in the Parent ego state of the child tapes that the child can play back later to himself. He is teaching the child how to heal his own psychological wounds, how to nurture himself. The wise parent, knowing the joy and effectiveness of a family able to give and receive love, conducts Adult-to-Adult conversations with members of the family in which stroking needs are discussed openly and unashamedly.

Permission to Be Yourself

From the permission to give and receive love comes the permission to be yourself. Erich Fromm says there are certain basic elements common to all forms of love, and they are *care, responsibility, respect,* and *knowledge.* He continues: "Responsibility could easily deteriorate into domination and possessiveness, were it not for a third component of love, *respect.* Respect is not fear and awe. . . . [It is] the ability to see a person as he is, to be aware of his unique individuality. Respect means the concern that the other person should grow and unfold as he is. . . . If I love the other person, I feel one with him or her, but with him *as he is,* not as I need him to be as an object for my use. It is clear that respect is possible only if I have achieved independence, if I can stand and walk without needing crutches, without having to dominate and exploit anyone else." *

The loving parent gives his child permission to be himself. This does not mean that he exercises no discipline, allows the child to run wild or even to ignore math. *Permission* is not the same as *permissiveness.* The child is not turned loose at a tender age and told by a neglectful parent, "Good luck with your motorcycle." Permission to be himself simply means that within the boundaries of his duties and his culture, the child has permission to enjoy and

*E. Fromm, *The Art of Loving* (New York: Harper & Row, 1956), p. 28.

respect what he is, that he has not been given harsh instructions which will basically alter his nature and make entire areas of his personality unavailable to him. Messages (implicit or explicit) to a child that would keep him from being himself are:

"Don't be a girl." ("When you were born I wanted a boy," etc. Girl is given boy's name, perhaps; is dressed boyishly.)

"Don't be a boy."

"Girls shouldn't go out for sports."

"Boys don't cry."

"Don't read so much."

"Don't laugh."

"Don't talk."

"Why can't you be more like your sister, or Goody Two-Shoes down the street?"

"You'll never amount to anything."

Butch, the Rum-Rum Kid

Butch's parents required that he be tough and daring. He was known as the "rum-rum kid" until the day he died. The neighborhood children in the small Midwestern town called him that because whenever they saw Butch he was imitating a motorcycle or car engine being revved up. He had been making that noise since he was three or four years old, when his parents put him on a bicycle that was too big for him and sent him off into the streets.

Butch's father was big on macho, he-man stuff. As a sometime daredevil, he occasionally picked up an odd dollar racing motorcycles or cars on weekends at run-down racetracks. The entire family was stroke-deprived and thought any display of affection was effeminate. The only way young Butch got any attention at all was by taking chances with his life.

By the age of ten, Butch had devised all sorts of "rum-rum" activities that would take him hurtling from high abutments, bounding down concrete stairways, and doing "wheelies" up and over ramps he had built. Whenever he saw kids his own age, his greeting was a challenge to see who would risk as much as he. Kids being kids, they would urge Butch on to greater and greater dares, and those not under the macho spell let Butch win and laughed at his foolish antics.

And so Butch grew. Big strokes followed big risks. The higher the ramp Butch jumped from, the more Butch's mother praised his daring. "You're just like your father," she told Butch. One day, during a new daredevil stunt, Butch fell off a four-foot ramp and cut off a finger. The praise for the now eleven-year-old reached a new high. Butch's older sister indicated the requirements of their household when she said, "Boy, that's some kid. He didn't even cry."

Nor did Butch whimper the day after his thirteenth birthday when a blameless driver struck him down as he raced a friend to see who would be first across a busy intersection. The friend, having little need to accumulate strokes for recklessness, was careful; Butch was not.

This true story is told not to prove how bad parents can be, but as an extreme example of the lengths children will go to for strokes from their parents. Butch got strokes for risking his life, another child gets strokes for getting straight A's, another for always pleasing Mother, or for always being perfect. In some households the children are given strong negative strokes for showing anger or resentment or for expressing any ideas of their own. Most stroking patterns in a family do not kill or maim, as Butch's did, but they do influence the child's future life. Children depend for survival on the giants in their life who take care of them. They learn what it takes to please the giants, even at the cost of their alive inner self.

My Son, the Dolt

Paul and Marie raised their son to be a dolt. They were so skilled in the matter, they could have given lessons in dolt-training. Their son, Rodney, was what is known in education as a "slow learner," meaning that as the child progresses in lock step through the system, he can't keep up with his classmates. Rodney could keep up with the universe all right in that he eventually learned to read, write, multiply, divide, and get along with others, but his own system often wasn't ready to handle the material at the same time as many of the other students. And let the student beware who falls outside the accepted norms; he can't be himself. Many of Rodney's teachers thought that teaching consisted of keeping accurate records of how far each student was falling behind, and so, with professional righteousness, they sent home with Rodney periodic "dolt" messages. "He doesn't grasp the material," "He is making insufficient progress," said the teachers in generalized phrases impossible to take effective action on, yet meaning very plainly to Rodney that he was not good enough as a human being. The system had other clever little tortures for Rodney. Many of the teachers, programmed on "Be neat and orderly" tapes, lined the children up according to size, smallest to largest. Here again, Rodney was wounded. He stood out as the largest—big, hulking, and dumb.

Paul and Marie should have fought the school "dolt" messages tooth and nail. Why allow an imperfect system, which should be essentially constructive, to put a label on their child that may hurt him the rest of his life? Instead, they joined with the teachers and told Rodney:

"You'll never learn."
"You're such an oaf."
"We might as well take you out of school."
"Why can't you get it through your thick head?"

There are many Rodneys in this world. Some, against incredible odds, make it, but many others become a burden on society, fighting a system that would not give them enough good strokes for healthy psychological survival. These children could be protected from "dolt" messages, whether they originate in the home or in the classroom. Many a teacher has encouraged a child to realize potential he never dreamed he had by setting up situations in which he can experience success. Other teachers don't seem to realize that often when a student gets an F, the *teacher* has flunked the course.

Permission to Be Joyful

Life can be perceived as either a privilege or a problem, and the difference between the two perceptions is not accounted for by luck. Many don't experience joy, not because their life is so difficult, but because there is little from which they derive satisfaction. Blessed with all fortune has to offer, they grumble their way through life and, like Miniver Cheevy, grow lean while they assail the seasons. On the other hand, Helen Keller, although blind and deaf, said, "I have found life so beautiful."

One family looks out on the strange planet they inhabit and tell themselves and their children that all they observe is a tragedy which sooner or later they must take part in, that everything is so desperate there is nothing to feel joyful about. Another family teaches the children that life itself is a gift, and although the stipulations are "Cinderella"-like and will end at midnight, there will still be a happy ending.

Life is meant to be celebrated and not guarded against. Children must have permission to be active and expressive, humorous, spontaneous, loving, high-spirited; they need permission to enjoy, to live. Our children need permission to be human, with all that implies. They need to be taught to give and receive love, that you can't label people, that mercy is as important as justice, that they must be trustworthy, in the full sense of the word, and treat others humanely. Much of this can be accomplished by the parents, some by the schools. Let's cut out dull, non-applicable, non-sense, "saber-toothed" curricula, and institute courses such as: Characteristics of a Human Being 1-A, Introduction to Giving and Receiving

Love, Humane Treatment of Self and Others, Advanced Seminar in the Practice of Joy. As people become more joyful, they become more human, which, in turn, leads to more joy.

You Must Please Mother

Janey was raised to believe: "You must always please Mother." She learned to think not about her own desires, but about her mother's wishes. As a child she received strokes only when she met her mother's demands completely. Any behavior at variance with what Mother wanted was met with disapproval and swift punishment. Janey's mother was a stern and rigid woman who ruled her joyless house with military precision, brooking no infractions. Janey's toilet training took only forty-eight hours, a tribute to her mother's iron will and a heartless technique suggested in a book written by a psychologist who may have been thinking more about royalties than about children.

Automatic obedience was demanded of Janey; she wasn't allowed to protest. She recalls one day when she was eight years old and invited to a beach picnic with her playmate's family. She wanted to wear the new bathing suit her grandmother had sent for her birthday. Her mother said no, and when Janey pleaded with her, her mother, sensing incipient disobedience, told Janey she couldn't even go and sent her to her room for the rest of the day.

As Janey grew older, things became more complicated. It wasn't enough to please Mother all the time by doing what she said. For a perfect score, she must *guess* what Mother wanted. She might get her mother's permission to stay after school for cheerleading practice, only to be met on her return home with icy silence. She was supposed to have guessed that Mother's acquiescence was that of a martyr, and a truly good, unselfish girl would have known her long-suffering mother needed her at home.

Janey's mother passed away ten years ago on a cold and sunless winter day, a victim to the end. Her last words to Janey were: "The soup you served me wasn't even hot." Janey still spends her psychic energy trying to satisfy the "You must please me" voice implanted in her brain. She doesn't realize it, but the first lightning-like thought that flashes through her mind before she undertakes any action is: "Will this please Mother?" Janey never considers asking herself what she wants from life, what she would like to do, what demands on her time are unreasonable. From time to time she makes pitiful attempts to assert herself, but retreats quickly, anxious that somehow she will be punished, something bad will happen.

Don't Think About Sex

John and Gloria forbade all mention of sex in their household, thereby guaranteeing that their children would be forever preoccupied with the subject. They put so much thought into how to keep their children from thinking about sex that it was the major unspoken topic in their home. It was on everyone's mind most of the time.

The children were under strict instructions to cover their eyes or ears whenever sex reared its ugly head on the television screen, on the radio, or in a movie. They were finely attuned even to the slightly suggestive. They couldn't see a couple kissing on the TV screen and casually ask someone to pass the popcorn. Kissing called for mobilization of the senses; something important was going on. Their early warning system must be ever alert so as not to miss the smallest hint of hanky-panky. Had John and Gloria been able to libidinize math in their children, creating the same exaggerated interest as they had in sex, they would have raised mathematical geniuses.

The "Don't think about sex" injunction ruined the oldest daughter's marriage. Her husband was raised in a family that talked openly about everything. Their only dirty-word list consisted of ethnic slurs. If any of the children used a prejudiced word or told a racial joke, there was hell to pay. Consequently, the husband was deeply hurt when he discovered he couldn't discuss sex with his wife and she informed him he had the foulest mouth she had ever heard.

John and Gloria's youngest son was arrested on a "peeping Tom" charge. Gloria said at the time, "I can't believe he did that. He sure didn't learn that at home."

Sometimes children rebel against parental instructions with opposite behavior, but there is no more freedom in compulsive rebellion than in compulsive compliance. Some people have been conditioned to think about sex every waking moment. There's a story about a psychologist who drew a straight line on a sheet of paper and asked his patient what it brought to his mind. "Sex," replied the patient. The psychologist then drew two straight lines on the paper and asked the patient what he associated that with. The patient replied again, "Sex." "Do you see how your mind is focused on sex?" asked the psychologist. "You can't hang that on me," answered the patient. "You're the one drawing all the dirty pictures."

Transacting with Your Teen-Ager

Many B-plus parents wonder, when their children become teenagers, if they aren't flunking completely as parents. The teen years can be difficult for the child, and they're often just as hard on the parents. Sometimes, in the strange way the passing of time manifests itself, it seems as if almost overnight the little boy or girl who grabbed Mommy's hand to go shopping or Daddy's hand to jump in the car and go anyplace, turns into a complete stranger in the house. One day you could please the child with the box the watch came in; the next day you can't please him with the watch. The change can be frightening. As the teen-ager goes about his mysterious errands, sometimes silent and uncommunicative, the anxious parent finds the change impossible to understand. He feels rebuffed, unappreciated, and unloved.

When the parent attempts to break through the child's protective shell, he meets with impatience and hostility, and the inevitable blowup occurs. The parent feels anger, followed by guilt, followed by resentment: "Why should I feel guilty when I give him everything he has?" This, in turn, leads to more conflict, driving the adolescent further away.

If the teen-ager is a trial to his parents, he is also a burden to himself. He is neither child nor adult. He is caught in a flood of emotions that sweep him first one way, then another. He wants the privacy and inner consultation that goes with maturity, yet desperately needs the understanding and love that only parents are willing to give. He longs to be protected, yet is compelled to seek independence. Like a young bird, he is driven to try wings that are not yet ready for flight. He is trying to find himself; still, he craves the approval of his peers. His mood swings can be as swift as the ups and downs of a roller-coaster ride.

Some parents torture themselves with an idealized picture of life as it *should* be: Daughter bursts in the front door, home from high school right on time, hangs up her clothes, quickly tidies her room, then hurries to the kitchen, hugs her mother, and says, "Mom, I want to tell you all about what happened today, but first I'll make biscuits for dinner tonight. It will make Brother so happy because he just loves them." We cause ourselves to suffer with these visions of the ideal family that exist only in our minds. There *are* moments to be treasured forever, but they are peaks that stand out on the horizon of day-to-day living. The best advice for parents in such a situation is simply this: Relax; stop trying so hard. Be gentle with yourself. Don't demand a level of expertise in handling young teen-agers that none of us achieves. One of the most important benefits of the various parent-training classes conducted around the country is the discovery that other parents are not perfect either. It's comforting to find that others are experiencing the same frustrations. It's not so much your performance that is in error as your expectations. Perhaps you're taking the antics and emotional swings of your teen-ager too seriously. Relax, come up to your Adult ego state, refuse to feel self-contempt for not being a perfect parent, ignore the Critical Parent voice within you that accuses you of failure.

Communicating with Your Children at Any Age

In Chapter 7, on communication, I discussed Creative Listening and its effectiveness in human relations. There is no situation in which Creative Listening is more desirable than in dealing with children of any age. If you refer to the Creative Listening section, you can apply those points in communicating with your children. In Creative Listening, we listen, accept what we hear, pass no judgments, but try to enter the world of the other person and see how things appear to him. With our children we try to hear their real needs and wants. We make it safe for them to tell us the truth. You can be sure, whether he is able to state it verbally or not, the young person needs love and appreciation. He needs good strokes in the form of praise for his accomplishments, and this doesn't mean you must wait until he wins the Nobel Prize. He can be praised for bringing a D to a C, for mowing the lawn, for dusting two rooms, for picking up his toys.

You may need to be an advanced practitioner of Creative Listening to hear your child ask for love. He may do it by testing you to your limits to see if you can truly love the terrible person he may think he is at the moment. A teen-ager, tossed in the tempest of emotions he does not understand, criticized by parents and teachers, failing a subject, cut from the team, bored by his studies, having no idea what to do with his life, can feel just terrible about himself. To give him love on such days takes the skill and courage of a pilot bombing a city protected by fighter planes. You may very well be shot down before reaching your target; if so, try another run.

Creative Listening, applied to the child, means you take his world seriously. Problems which to him are devastating may seem minor from your vantage point of experience and years, but they must not be treated as minor. Grades, just for one example, mean nothing once a person emerges from the academic pipeline; yet just a few years back, a college student in Tallahassee, Florida, failed an exam and because of this, it is believed, went home and killed himself. Each year, according to author Francine Kalgsbrun in *Too Young To Die*, as many as 400,000 young people may attempt suicide. Their problems must not be dismissed, with a wave of the hand, as "childish."

Disclose Your Feelings

In Chapter 11, on marriage, we discussed the "I feel" method of communication. It works with children too. The object here is to tell the child how you *feel* about his behavior, and to avoid making accusations or judgments about him. You start by saying "I feel," rather than "You are."

Accusation	Communication
You never practice your guitar. You're wasting good money on lessons. I have told you and told you, but you don't care because you're too selfish.	I feel as if we're wasting money on guitar lessons when you don't practice.
You're late again. You are never once on time What's the matter with you?	I feel worried when you're not home at the time we agreed on.
Your taste in music is rotten. How can you stand that awful noise? Kids nowadays don't have any sense at all.	I feel nervous when you play your music so loud. It's not my kind of music, but it's all right if you keep it down.
You are so lazy, you wouldn't care if I was ready to drop. You never offer to help.	I feel very tired tonight. Would you help me finish this job?

It's not always easy for a parent to get at his real feelings and state them instead of resorting to accusations. When Johnny refuses to pick up a magazine because "Suzy read it last," after you have spent hours chauffeuring him to various lessons and amusements, it's difficult not to call the kid "ingrate" and "slob" and work your way down from there. The more effective way, though, is to tell the child that by giving him your time and effort, you are showing your love, and you feel that he doesn't appreciate you. Once again, don't expect the scenario to go the way it does in some of the child-rearing manuals. He may very well not rush up to you and say, "Gee, Mom, I love you, and I'm sorry I behaved selfishly." But the child will know where you stand, how you really feel, and he will not conclude that you consider him a low and contemptible person.

The child, when he is old enough to reason, can be taught Transactional Analysis* so that he can understand himself, his parents, his teachers, and others in his life. The parents can maintain a home atmosphere in which discussion and dissent are permitted. The child who questions and disagrees is developing his Adult. It's a lucky parent who has taught his child to stay in his Adult ego state during an argument and help his parent who has lost his temper. Parents have told me, and I agree, it's a thrilling experience to hear your son or daughter say, "Dad, I think you're on tapes. Let's discuss this Adult to Adult."

To listen to your child creatively, to disclose your ego states and tell him how you feel, requires that you spend time with him alone,

*Teach your child the basics of Transactional Analysis. Tell him about his three ego states and his three self-feelings (Chapter 4). TA is a psychology that can be presented so that even very young children can understand it. Teachers can grasp TA quickly and then teach it to their students. Mentally healthy, self-reliant young citizens have long been a goal of educators, but they seldom know, specifically, where to start, other than a high-sounding statement of human goals in the school catalogue. TA is a start. Many school systems are finding TA a practical, effective method to teach young people how to understand themselves and others, easy and inexpensive to introduce into the curriculum. Taxpayers, when they see the catalogue promise: "to develop well-rounded citizens who understand themselves and the world they live in" become a reality are bound to be impressed.

away from the other children, away from your spouse. It's not the quantity, but the quality of time that counts. Refuse to be distracted, focus on the child, listen to him, and put your own problems out of your mind. Some openers are: "What's the best thing that's happened to you lately?" "Who is your best friend now? Why do you like him?" "What is your biggest worry?" "What scares you most of all?" Remember this is not the time for recorded announcements, but time to absorb the reality of this young human being who will be on his own before you know it.

When the child is old enough—and as a concerned parent you'll know when this is and will need no expert to tell you—share your humanity with him. Gradually share some of your hopes and fears. You and I both know I don't mean to scare him. You want him to feel secure. But it's much better to sit the child down and tell him that Dad just lost his job and that's why he's so irritable than to try to keep it a secret and end up with the youngster thinking he has done something wrong. Tell him Dad got fired. It was unfair, but things will be all right because Dad's a fighter and never gives up. The two rules to follow here are Truth (it doesn't have to be the *whole* truth) and Ability To Process. You can give the child as much truth as you, the parent, think he can process without distortion. As the child grows older, it's important that he view you as a human, not as a critical robot, and realize that you, too, experience fear, hurt, and frustration.

Reward Warm, Communicative Behavior Quickly

Do you remember how good your inner Child felt the last time you got a stroke? The chances are you couldn't wait to repeat the behavior to get that stroke again. We're all like that. Remember this the next time your young child or teen-ager opens up to you and communicates something pleasing, or troubling, his innermost heart. These are some of the moments we treasure most in life. Reward this behavior immediately and, like the rest of us, the child will want to repeat it. Drop everything and listen with your full attention. Put yourself in the place of the child and look at what he's talking about the way he looks at it. Then perhaps you hold each other for a moment, or go for a walk, or bake a cake together, or make an extra big submarine sandwich for his lunch. Maybe later you even ask him to advise you on a problem you're having.

It's OK to Fight

Children must be allowed to own and express their feelings of anger, fear, resentment, envy. Forbidding these feelings will accomplish nothing except to drive them underground. The child must be taught not to hit his little sister, but it's all right to be angry with her. When he says he hates her, the parent might help him to define his feelings more precisely by asking, "Do you mean you don't like her right now because she ate all the cookies?" Children can be helped to understand that feelings are ambivalent and often fleeting, and there is no reason to feel guilty about them.

Many parents tell me that when their children fight, it sends them right up the wall. Even catching one child glaring at another with pure malice sends their blood pressure up. A father of four said he has delivered stirring speeches about family unity, brothers and sisters facing the world shoulder to shoulder. The children thoroughly enjoy the lectures and go right back to fighting. Another father told about coming home after a particularly hard day at the office, with dissension and disagreements among the employees, and he blew his stack when the kids began to argue. Then he said he saw the irony of expecting kids to get along in perfect harmony when adults can't get along with each other even when their livelihood depends on it.

There's a solution to the sibling fight problem that's fairly simple once we give ourselves three permissions:

1. The children have permission to fight (no hurting allowed).
2. The parents have permission to get angry about it.

3. The parents have permission to mete out reasonable punishment.

The permissions recognize and accept the fact that siblings will fight, parents will get upset about it, and punishments will follow. This solution invariably reduces family friction because the fights, given sanction, lose their importance. The parents do not reinforce the fighting by giving it great emotional significance, and unproductive guilt feelings are eliminated. It's important that the punishments be reasonable—a day's grounding, an extra turn doing dishes—so that the parents will follow through with it since it's not too harsh.

Remember the Apology

While we're on the subject of arguments, let's remember the soothing, healing effect of an apology. The best way to teach your child to apologize is by apologizing to *him* when you are wrong. The B-plus parent can do this because he doesn't need to defend perfection in himself. He can comfortably admit he was wrong. In a disagreement with his child, the parent can often sense when he has overstated his case, move into (cathect) his Adult ego state, and say to the child: "Son, I was on tapes just now when I chewed you out. Forgive me." Or: "Daughter, I was wrong; I overreacted to what was really a small mistake on your part. I'm sorry." Don't worry that you will lose face in the sight of your child for doing this. Most children, by the time they are nine or ten, already know about the imperfections of human beings, including their parents. But they are unaccustomed to a grownup being so sure of himself that he can admit he is wrong.

It's OK to Be Different

Many parents don't realize that it's OK for their child to be different from other children, different from the way the parents were when they were children. One father told me he was very worried about his son because he acted so different. I asked him what was so unusual about the boy's behavior. He said, "He wants to read all the time. He doesn't go out for sports; he's not interested in athletics like I was when I was a boy."

Several parents have told me they worry when their teen-age boy or girl shows no interest in the opposite sex. Many of their worries on this subject are groundless. Some children mature much later than others; others are interested, but just don't let their parents know it. E. B. White, in *The Second Tree from the Corner,* tells with his usual humor how hidden and subtle a teen-ager's interest in the opposite sex may be: ". . . nevertheless, she was the girl I singled out, at one point, to be of special interest to me. Being of special interest to me involved practically nothing on a girl's part —it simply meant that she was under constant surveillance."*

Children don't need to be athletes, or A students, or popular. None of these goals that parents often have for their children guarantees anything for the child's future. The child who is allowed to find his own interests, to pursue his goals without feeling parental tension, to discover the music within himself, is the child most likely to find happiness.

As he grows older, the child may have some questions about his parents' religious beliefs. If the questions are in his mind, they might as well be out in the open to answer. The Judeao-Christian religions have been around a long time and have withstood questioning by scholars. Some children get the impression that their Creator can't stand too much scrutiny. Parents whose religion is intrinsic, who are strengthened and sustained by it, will tell the child what they believe in, what they have a commitment to, and will encourage questions from the child that will fortify his Adult against future cynicism.

*E. B. White, *The Second Tree from the Corner* (New York: Harper & Brothers, 1954), pp. 17–18.

Give Your Child That Winning Feeling

Some psychologists maintain that all of us become the sum total of what significant others in our life thought we were. We receive a constant flow of what Dr. Harry Stack Sullivan calls "reflected appraisals." The parents, teachers, and friends in a child's life define him to himself, and his self-definition then determines what he will be. Research shows that if the parents and teachers of a child treat him as backward, slow to learn, and a D student, then the child acts backward, is slow to learn, and gets D's. What others expect of us becomes a self-fulfilling prophecy.

In an interesting experiment, teachers were told that the students they were to teach were exceptionally bright A students. Sure enough, at the end of the marking period, the students got all A's. The truth is they had never been A students at all; the teachers were just told this to see what would happen. Humans, being what we are, treat "bright" students differently than average or dull students. Let a bright student ask a stupid question, and the teacher is convinced there must be a deep meaning to the question. Experimenters even treat "bright" rats differently than they do the dull ones. Research conducted on researchers themselves shows that the maze-wise rates—i.e., those that consistently find their way through the maze faster than average—are held longer by the researchers, petted more, given more pellets, etc.

Children must be told that those who get C grades, whether in the classroom or in something else in life, are not C people. The child who gets C this year may excel in other subjects at other times, or in other challenges. The child should be given a large collection of tapes in his head that will play automatically and nurture and encourage him when things go wrong. They will be with him all through his life when he needs them, saying:

"Forget it; you did the best you could."
"Everybody makes mistakes sometimes."
"You can always give it another try."
"You're doing a great job; don't worry."

Praise the child and help him feel like a winner. Sure, he has to be corrected and controlled; he must be taught not to play with matches, not to steal, and not to hurt people. He must learn about duty and discipline, telling the truth, brushing his teeth, doing his homework, and finishing his chores. But we don't have to focus on his shortcomings. The best way to prepare a child to meet the world is not by damaging his self-concept. He won't learn to be a winner by feeling like a loser. Homes and schools should be set up so the child feels like a winner and OK about himself. Tell him *specifically* what he is doing well. Say, "Boy, you sure did a good job trimming the bushes around the house" or "I admire the way you buckled down and brought your math grade from a D to a C. Winners experience small victories, feel good about themselves, and go on to bigger victories.

13

How to Go From "Down" to "Up"

This chapter is not for the seriously depressed person, incapacitated or long-suffering. He should be helped by reading this, but needs more than a book can give. If you or a loved one is deeply depressed, please get professional help. I personally favor TA therapy, but only you can decide who to see. You might first find it wise to check with your family doctor to rule out a physical cause.

It puzzles me why people hesitate to seek professional help for mental or emotional illness. Such illness is more painful than are many injuries to the body. Yet emotional and mental pain of a magnitude that would induce someone to rush to a doctor if it were caused by physical injury is simply endured by the sufferer. I suspect one reason the depressed person doesn't seek help is his feeling of hopelessness. He thinks there is no help available for his dismal situation. How, he asks himself, could a therapist give him back a loved one, find him a better job, repair a broken body, change the shrew he's married to, make him younger, or do anything to change his existential position. He's right that therapy can't change reality. But it can bring about almost miraculous change in the way he perceives and reacts to reality, and it can enable the sufferer's mind to function so that he can solve his problems. Depression is a malady that yields to treatment in the hands of a professional.

Another reason the depressed person doesn't want to seek help might be his fear of the cost of such treatment, especially if money is one of his worries to begin with. TA practitioners, for the most part, work with people in groups, and this keeps the cost down. In addition, Transactional Analysis gives insights to help you right away, in the present.

This chapter, as is the rest of the book, is written for so-called normal people who want to become more effective, who want to have more control over their "down" days, who want to handle their moods better and conquer joylessness. As Shakespeare said: "And such a want-wit sadness makes of me, that I have much ado to know myself." Let's see if we can know ourselves better and use the knowledge anytime we wish to go from "down" to "up."

Dean and the Three Chairs*

A thirty-nine-year-old student I'll call Dean told me one evening after a TA class that he had felt "down" and mildly depressed for a number of years, not so bad that he couldn't work or attend school, but enough so that he found life tasteless and dull to the spirit. I had noticed Dean earlier during the course because he never smiled. During class breaks he seldom mingled with other students, but stood in a corner of the student lounge somberly drinking his coffee.

While we talked that evening, Dean told me that for the first time in his life he felt what he was doing to himself. It had happened earlier in the evening when I set out three chairs in front of the class and asked for a volunteer to demonstrate how you might get in touch with the different parts of your personality. Dean, surpris-

* The chairs technique, in a slightly different form, was originated by Dr. Frederick Perls.

ingly, volunteered and I was quick to choose him, knowing the chances were good this exercise would help the serious, unsmiling student.

I asked Dean to sit in the chair labeled Child and, ignoring the class as much as possible, tell his feeling, if he wished, about a particular problem in his life. Dean exhibited no self-consciousness and entered into the exercise with apparent ease. "To tell the truth," he said, "I feel bad about life in general. My head often feels like it's in a vise, or full of heavy water that won't let me break through its surface and enjoy myself. I haven't experienced enthusiasm for anything for nine, ten years. I go through the rote of living, selling, and running my real estate office, raising a family, coming here to school, but it's all mechanical."

After Dean had gone on like this for several minutes, I asked him to switch to the Parent chair, facing the Child chair, and tell what one of his parents might say to the Child through which Dean had just spoken. Dean sat in the Parent chair and said, "I can hear my father now and what he would say." I then told Dean not to *hear* his father, but *be* his father and talk to the Child in the opposite chair. Dean started out: "Son, you'll never amount to anything. Here you sit again feeling sorry for yourself. Why the hell don't you quit sucking for sympathy, get off your butt, and work harder? Why the hell don't you try harder? Be a man, get hold of yourself. The hell with sympathy, boy; try success." This went on for several minutes, with Dean's Parent openly criticizing his Child, until I asked Dean to respond to the Parent from the Child's chair.

Dean's face changed in the Child's chair, as did his gestures. As the Parent, Dean's face had been stern, unyielding, filled with disgust and anger. As the Child, Dean's face softened, and his gestures implored rather than threatened. "Get off my back, will you? I'm doing the best I can. I wish to holy hell I could succeed, as you call it, but I'm trying as hard as I know how. Damn it, I'm trying and trying and trying."

"Trying, hell," said Dean from the Parent chair. "You're a damned goof-off and you always have been. Since when did you put out full effort on anything? I'm damned sick of you. Wish to hell I never had a child."

This continued for a few more minutes. It's always surprising to those who have not worked in human relations how some people can get up in front of others and let their feelings out. Yet this is often the way to peace of mind, and I'm convinced that many know intuitively that if they can make themselves transparent, they will find healing in the process.

Finally, I asked Dean to sit in the third chair, which was at right angles to the other two, and from this, the Adult chair, give the wisest counsel he could to the Child and to the Parent. At first, as often happens, there was only silence. If our ears were equipped to tune into the minds of others during this silence, we would hear the grinding and stripping of gears as the personality shifts from Child feelings to Parent opinions and criticism to the Adult mode with its information and objectivity. Sometimes it's the first time in a person's entire life that he has been ordered—no, given *permission*—to *think* about what he has been doing to himself. It's the first time he experiences awareness of his three selves.

"Well," Dean said, "I would like to talk to the Child first and tell him this: 'You're a fine little guy, and if anyone knew how hard you're working to please that monster [pointing to the Parent chair], they would give you a damn medal.' " Then Dean calmed down into his Adult ego state. Still looking at the Child chair, he said: "You know, considering the cards you've been dealt, you've done a good job. You have a business; sure, times are tough, but you'll make it. Your wife loves you. You work every day. Your trouble is you feel like you're under a smothering blanket because you're trying so hard to do the impossible. God knows you try." With the word "try," Dean, who could evidently feel how hard the Child had been trying, broke down and cried unashamedly. When he finished I gently motioned him toward the Child chair, praying that Dean had at last got in touch with the fine Child he, like the rest of us, has hidden inside—often subjugated, tormented, and beaten down by a merciless inner voice that is out of touch with reality and always dissatisfied. Sympathy for the suffering inner self (or Child) is essential to mental health.

Later, back in the Adult chair, Dean looked at the Parent chair and said very calmly: "I think you're much too hard on the boy. He's not doing too badly, you know. Why not take it a little easier on him? If you let him up, you might be surprised at what he'll accomplish. But great accomplishments or not, he'll get some enjoyment out of life." Then, turning to the Child, Dean said: "Stop feeling as if you must please that inner voice, that inner urge. It's only in your head. It's a toothless tiger. You have my permission to feel good about yourself."

Dean benefited greatly from his insight into the war going on within himself. His Adult was strong enough to recognize the force that caused his depression. For perhaps the first time in his life, he felt his real feelings. Several weeks after our course concluded, Dean joined a TA therapy group, and the trained therapist gave him powerful protection to further ignore the Critical Voice that had been keeping him down.

A Self-Induced Malady

You get down and discouraged because you beat on yourself. It's something you do to yourself to bring about the feeling. Freud said depression is anger turned inward. The exceptions to this are endogenous depression, caused by an internal malfunction of the nervous system, and existential grief over a severe loss, such as the death of a loved one. Even grief, however, should recede and lose its force over a period of time; if it doesn't, here again, you are keeping yourself depressed.

But by far the majority of those suffering from what they call "the blues," "down" days, feelings of discouragement, and even depression have caused it, however unwittingly, themselves. It is a malady that is self-induced.

This does not mean that self-caused depression is any less distressing or enervating than if it were caused by outside forces; it is just as real misery as any other kind. If you purposely infected yourself, the disease that racked your body would be just as real as if an insect had infected you. It should give hope, however, to know its self-induced nature. After all, if you're not the victim of outside forces, and it's something going on within you, then you can feel hopeful that it is in your power to end it. You can conquer these self-inflicted feelings if you are willing to work at it.

Conditional Living

In Chapter 4 we talked about our Child feelings and said that many people live *conditional* lives. They do not feel they are OK; they feel they are OK *if. If* is the big word here, and they will never understand themselves until they understand the conditional lease on life they are living under.

They feel OK *if* they do everything better than anyone else.
They feel OK *if* they are liked by everyone.
They feel OK *if* they make a lot of money.
They feel OK *if* people make a fuss over them.
They feel OK *if* they make no mistakes.

OK If people give themselves conditional approval for living. They have a lease on life cancellable on a moment's notice. The inner judge, the Critical Parent, sits merciless and disapproving, ready to flood the personality with self-contempt unless unrealistic standards are met. Accomplishments are ignored by the inner judge. It has no real interest in accomplishments. Its main purpose is to keep the personality under strain, tension, and stress, always striving for the ever-elusive goal of approval. Unfortunately, these unrealistic self-expectations are often given the name "ambition." But the person who drives himself unmercifully, trying to save time and make no mistakes, is not effective, and he may bring on a physical or emotional illness. The outstanding characteristics of

effective people are: they set moderate goals possible of achievement, they work at a relaxed pace, they allow a margin of time for
the inevitable delays, and they expect a reasonable amount of
mistakes. OK If people do not allow themselves to live this way.

How You Get Yourself Down

Conditional living can be distilled to this three-step method for
getting yourself depressed. It's guaranteed and seldom fails.

1. You set up unrealistic goals or claims on life. (The Critical
Parent says you may like yourself if you achieve perfection.)

2. Because they are unrealistic claims, you will inevitably fall
short.

3. You blame yourself. (Your Child is flooded with self-contempt, and you lock in to your automatic bad feeling.)

Day in, day out, back and forth the personality goes, trying to
appease the Critical Parent, unable to achieve perfection, down
again into self-contempt. A promotion, an election, a raise, a spotless house, a triumph, and the person is allowed temporary relief,
but then the voice is back: "What have you done superhuman for
me lately?" and another matchless performance is called for.

How You Keep Yourself Down

Once you get yourself down, you are likely to *keep* yourself
down. Here are three ways you may work against yourself:

1. When you have contempt for yourself, you naturally don't
love yourself. When you don't love yourself, you behave in an
unlovable way and attract negative strokes from others.

2. Your feeling of hopelessness keeps you immobilized. Since you
feel nothing can help you, you don't want to get out and take
positive steps to help yourself.

3. You lie to yourself. When you feel down, you shade everything
darker than it really is. Slanting the truth just a little here and a
little there can make all the difference.

How to Get Up

Now that you know what causes you to get down, it's easier to learn how to get up. Your self-blame sentences will alert you. You hear yourself saying: "I *should* have," "I *ought* to," "How dumb can I be," "I'll never learn," "Always blundering," etc., and you know you're abusing your inner Child. You can *feel* your own feelings and have some sympathy for yourself. You can say to that demand for perfection: "I don't have to be perfect. I can just do well. Or I can just do."

You get up and stay up by putting your Adult in charge of your personality. Chances are you have spent most of your life practicing your automatic bad feeling. Depression, hopelessness, joylessness, and discouragement are the feelings that many have chosen as a response to the Critical Voice that beats on their Child. The response can be so sensitive that the slightest mistake or a disapproving look from a stranger can trigger it. Depression, unless it's physical, is a *learned* response. If you suspect your depression is caused, even partially, by a physical problem, see a medical doctor. A clean bill of health means you can no longer sabotage your efforts to avoid depression by telling yourself it's beyond your control.

Then make a decision that you are not going to practice that "racket feeling" anymore. (See "The Powerful Adult Goes Straight . . ." in Chapter 3.) *You* have caused *you* to suffer long enough, and now *you* are going to do something about it. Is it really that simple? Yes, the decision is that simple, but enforcing it takes practice. You have spent years learning to get yourself down, and it will take some effort to break that habit. You may have to redecide it every day. Some of my students have told me they had to redecide it several times a day, but finally the Adult becomes strong enough to take charge when the Critical Voice starts beating the Child into its old joyless feeling. So don't be discouraged if you find it difficult at first. You don't want to become depressed because you are not overcoming your depression perfectly.

How Your Adult Can Protect Your Child from Depression

1. Your Adult knows you have no immunity from cause and effect. The Child harbors a secret belief in its own omnipotence, but the Adult knows, although a positive outlook on life is necessary, that there are some variables over which a person has little or no control.

2. Your Adult insists on realistic, achievable goals, rewarding the Child when the goal is reached, and then setting another realistic goal. The Adult shields the Child from condemnation for failure to accomplish an objective so the Child will not be fearful of trying again.

3. Your Adult knows that feelings are not all-powerful unless we allow them to be. The Adult does not live in awe of the feelings of the discouraged or depressed Child within. The Adult knows: "It's only a feeling, and *feelings* are not *facts.*"

4. Your Adult refuses to accept the Child's pretensions because it will result in alienation from the real self. If the Child is allowed to arrogate to himself qualities he does not in reality possess, he will have to defend his fraudulence. The Adult motto is: "Pretend little, defend little." Accept and love your real self.

5. Your Adult defines and interprets accurately, not allowing the Child to take over in panic. The Adult distinguishes between disappointment and disaster. When a person is very "down" and discouraged, it may be that the personality is not so much emotionally sick as cognitively wrong.

6. Your Adult knows that stroke deprivation causes depression (see Chapter 5). People suffering from depression sometimes recover rapidly when they start receiving love, attention, and praise. One way to ensure an unlimited supply of good strokes is to give yourself strokes. If you had loving parents you will have a good supply of self-strokes in your Nurturing Parent. If you didn't, remember that self-respect and self-love are gifts you bestow on yourself.

7. Your Adult puts mental health first. The Adult knows that

exercise (permitted by your doctor), recreation, satisfying work, and adequate rest are all essential to active, happy, and healthful living.

8. The religious Adult prays because he believes in Something Beyond that can help him. The nonreligious Adult who believes there's nothing beyond can meditate to commune with himself. It will give him a better perspective.

9. Your Adult gives you permission to live, love, take personal risks for growth, handle setbacks and humiliations, ignore the Critical Parent, experience joy. It refuses to be vanquished.

10. Your Adult knows the word "depression" covers a complex set of feelings. You have to get around the word and see what's behind it. "I am depressed" does not express the real Child feelings. This may seem strange to you at first, but when your Child is depressed, often the heart of the problem is that your Child feels unloved or unlovable. "Depression" is a label that is not operational. It masks what is really happening. Your Adult figures out *why* the Child feels unloved or unlovable and sets about correcting it.

11. The Adult removes the "if." The Child within says, "I like myself *if.*" The Adult says, "I like myself."

14

A New Way
to Conquer Worry

The chances are you have already read several books telling you how to stop worrying, and yet keep right on doing so. It's a universal human malady. I'm not going to tell you how unproductive the habit is, how it can harm your health, destroy relationships, cause misery and stress; you undoubtedly know that. But I *am* going to give you a new way to attack worry. And this way will work for you if you practice it. Make an Adult contract with yourself (this is a procedure encouraged by many TA practitioners) to reread this chapter every time you start to worry for the next month. Don't underestimate the power of worry just because the word "worry" doesn't have academic standing or a Latin derivation. Worry, simply put, destroys people.

The first thing you must keep in mind about worry—and continue to remind yourself of this—is that worry is something *you do to yourself.* Do not say, "I have a worry problem," because that makes it sound like something outside yourself, apart from you. What is accurate to say is: "There are times when I choose to worry."

It's important you have no confusion on this. Your Adult must know that worry is something that you do to you. One part of you starts a worry tape from your favorite worry collection, and another part of you decides to let it play and listens to it.

Worry happens when your inner communication goes wrong. But it is you who allow it to go wrong. If you remember that you are three people in one, that you have three modes, you can get at your worry and anxiety problem.

It happens like this. During any particular minute of the day or night, your Parent may be hanging around with nothing in particular to do and makes a casual remark such as, "I wouldn't be surprised if that pain is heart trouble" or "I'll bet that bad break yesterday will be followed by more tough luck tomorrow." Your Child glances quickly around, notices the absence of the Adult, and lets out a yell: "Good grief, I think you're right. This is only the beginning; things are going to get much worse. Tell me again how bad it might be."

Your Child can be like a nervous horse. It is easily spooked. And once spooked, it will draw up mental images that will scare you to death, much as the Ghost told Hamlet it could do:

> I could a tale unfold whose lightest word
> Would harrow up thy soul; freeze thy young blood;
> Make thy two eyes, like stars, start from their spheres;
> Thy knotted and combined locks to part,
> And each particular hair to stand on end
> Like quills upon the fretful porcupine.
>
> *Hamlet,* Act I, Scene 5.

When you worry, it means that your inner Child ego state has taken control of your personality and is listening to frightening tapes with the volume turned on high. Sometimes you listen to these tapes over and over, and they become very familiar to you. They often frighten you into immobility. Tapes that have as their theme "What if" are particularly scary:

"What if I make a mistake?"
"What if I fail?"

"What if I get sick?"
"What if I lose my money?"
"What if I'm lonely?"
"What if they don't like me?"
"What if I can't do it?"

Why Do We Worry?

We worry for one, or several, of the following reasons:

We were taught to worry.

Many of us learned in childhood that the first thing to do about a problem or mishap is to worry about it. We believe this is the normal human reaction and can't imagine that some people merely shrug their shoulders over things that we worry about. If our parents worried about money, status, job security, respectability, health, then we are likely to worry about the same things in the same way. We'll repeat the same worry words and phrases they used. Worry habits are passed down from generation to generation like family heirlooms.

Many of us have been taught so well how to worry that we feel guilty when we don't. If we don't worry about life, we feel as if we're not "minding the shop" as we should. After all, we think, worrying means you're conscientious, and it keeps things from getting out of control. If you worry because you learned to worry, then you can also learn not to worry.

We may be under a "Don't think" injunction.

Some of us do not permit ourselves to *think* about our problems in a realistic and constructive way. We have developed the habit of confusing our mind and allowing our Child ego state to take over and merely fret about the problem, endlessly repeating it over and over. Sometimes we worry over a little problem so we won't think about something that bothers us even more.

We May be Fearful of Taking Action.

If we are fearful of taking action, or making a decision about a problem, we may hide these feelings from ourselves by worrying about the problem. "After all," we tell ourselves, "my worrying shows I'm doing something about the problem, doesn't it?"

We May Not be Busy Enough.

Many of us worry because we simply don't have enough to think about. Remember the old joke about the man who found his wife's lover hiding in the closet? When the husband demanded to know what he was doing there, he replied, "Everybody's got to be someplace, man." Well, the mind has to be someplace, and if you don't keep yourself active, interested, moving ahead, planning, setting goals, then it's going to find something to keep it busy. Worry is the occupation of the mind when it retires from life.

We Worry to Work Off Guilt

There's a long, involved explanation for why we worry to work off guilt. Very simply, it works like this: We feel guilty about something we did or did not do. We were raised to believe that if you are guilty of something, you should be punished, you should suffer. What better way to punish yourself when you feel guilty than to cause yourself to worry?

The TA Way to Conquer Worry

If you read the following ideas every day for the next two weeks and practice what they say, then you will be well on your way to conquering your worry habit. But don't miss a day. Remember, you have been practicing the habit of worry for a lifetime. Make a decision now to rid yourself of this life-destroying habit.

• When you start to worry, force yourself into your Adult ego state. State precisely what you are worried about. Define your problem; then list in your mind, or on a piece of paper, the possible solutions.

• Ask yourself whether what you're worried about would be a real disaster, a disappointment, or merely disagreeable. Learn to distinguish between the three.

• Practice turning the volume down on your worry tapes. There are different ways to do this. Try diverting yourself—go to a movie, exercise vigorously (if your health permits; this alone often causes worry to disappear), play your favorite music, buy a new hat, etc.

• Practice substituting a worry tape with a happy-fantasy tape. It's just as realistic to fantasize a sunny day tomorrow as flood conditions. For the first few weeks keep a humorous or interesting or inspiring book around. The minute you start to worry, pick it up and read awhile.

• Listen closely to your worry tape and picture yourself as a brilliant defense attorney arguing against what it is telling you. Notice how the tape slants the truth just a little bit on the negative side, try to catch it leaving out important bits of information, see how it eliminates hope completely. Argue out loud against it. State what you think is realistic.

• Free yourself of useless guilt. If you've done something you're truly ashamed of, do what you can to make amends, then forget about it. Fight back. Guilt places you in the past, and that's no place to live.

• Drop all pretensions. Remember we said, "Pretend little, defend little." If you stop all role-playing and pretending to be an A-plus person, you won't have to worry that people will find out you're not perfect, the same as the rest of us.

• Override the Parent Voice with your Adult. Tell it you have decided not to worry, that you do not think it is the conscientious thing to do. I want to tell you here in all capital letters, and I want you to hear me and remember what I say: YOU ARE NOT BEING CONSCIENTIOUS BY WORRYING, NOR ARE YOU PREPARING YOURSELF FOR THE FUTURE BY WORRYING. WORRY HAS NO VALID FUNCTION IN YOUR LIFE.

• Do not allow your "what if" tapes to play. If you start to worry "What if . . . What if," slam a compartment down in your mind to separate the present from all your tomorrows, and get very busy in the here and now. No more "what if"'s for the simple reason they can drive you, me, anybody, up the wall.

• Firmly decide there is no way you can solve tomorrow's problems with today's worry. "Take . . . no thought for the morrow. . . . Sufficient unto the day is the evil thereof" (Matthew 6:34).

• Come to grips with existential anxiety about the human condition. Remember: "Cowards die many times before their deaths;/-The valiant never taste of death but once" (*Julius Caesar,* Act II, Scene 2).

• Don't let your Child spook you. Don't believe the Child when it tells you that bad must always turn to worse.

• Don't ever retire from life. Keep busy. Make plans. Set goals. Refuse to believe the myths about aging.

• Remember, when you are tired or sick, your Adult can be more easily overwhelmed by your Critical Parent or your fearful Child. Refuse to take yourself seriously during these times. When you're prowling around the house at four in the morning, all alone, don't think about your problems.

• If you're caught in an argument or conflict, or your Child gets hostile with someone, realize that this often causes exaggerated uneasiness because the Child fears punishment, since this is what happened when you were small. Remember this, and your Adult will recognize irrational worry over a disagreement.

• Ask yourself if your worry is caused by an underlying Not OK feeling, if you sort of feel: "I'm inferior and I'm worried that I'll fail, or people will find out, or I'll make a fool of myself," etc. Take charge and remember that indulging the Not OK feeling of your inner Child is an incorrect way to live. Come back to your I'm OK —You're OK decision.

15

Autonomy: You're Only a Decision Away

The Almost Life

There are many of us who lead an "almost" life; we never quite make it to joy. We don't miss it by much. We are busy, often successful, keeping a house running smoothly, engaged in a profession, working for an organization, running a business. There is often not much negative in our life. We have few problems that amount to anything; and yet . . . and yet, we don't quite make it. We *almost* become winners, but something holds us back.

Some of us live Until lives. We decide we won't let go and be happy "until." The "until" can be anything, and once one "until" is satisfied, another takes its place. We decide we won't be happy until: I get married, I get divorced, all politicians become honest, inflation ends, I get a new house, I graduate, I get a promotion, sister moves out, everybody loves me, there is no more prejudice, my ship comes in. People expert at Until can immediately replace one "until" with another. The doctor's examination releases them from waiting to live until they find they don't have ulcers, and then, driving home from his office, they quickly dissipate their happiness

194

with their old "until"s. They're back again waiting to live until they have more money, position, power, or prestige.

Others of us play "I'm Going to Die Anyhow," so what's the use entering into life wholeheartedly. We think if we don't enjoy life too much it won't be so hard to give it up, that it's easier to die a thousand little deaths than one big one. But there is truly, as the Old Testament writer said, "a time to weep and a time to laugh," and a life lived half-heartedly is no life at all. You can't get a good grip on anything, including life, with your fingers crossed.

I'm Overwhelmed by Contradictions

Many allow themselves to be overwhelmed by the apparent contradictions they see in life. Rather than use their intelligence to sort things out, they give up. We all know there is a terrible conflict between competition and brotherly love. And who has not felt at times as if he had unlimited power to achieve his goals, then later gone to the other extreme and felt helpless? It's true that much of life is puzzling. It's like a fairy tale in which, if you kiss the frog, it turns into a prince. We have just two choices, really. We can either curse the rules for not making sense to us, or play the game and behold a prince. We must allow the conflicting thoughts into our mind and examine them, and not allow the Child within to block our thinking. Winners balance the contradictions in their mind, and much like a tightrope walker swaying this way and that, keep moving forward. If possible, they see the humor surrounding everyday situations. The lucky ones, like Scaramouche, are born with a gift of laughter and a sense that the world is mad.

You Can Let Go

In *The Varieties of Religious Experience,* William James relates a story which he said was often told by revivalist preachers of ". . . a man who found himself at night slipping down the side of a precipice. At last he caught a branch which stopped his fall, and remained clinging to it in misery for hours. But finally his fingers had to loose their hold, and with a despairing farewell to life, he let himself drop. He fell just six inches."

That's often the position you and I are in. We hang on for dear life to our fears, tensions, and anxieties. We become obsessed with "precautions that cannot shelter and safeguards that never save," as James said. All we need do is let go, and we'll fall but six inches to the solid ground of personal freedom. If we put our Adult ego state in charge of our lives to monitor, examine, and give appropriate play to the other ego states, we can find that freedom. By exercising that one discipline, we create a new world for ourselves.

Take Charge of Your Life

To take charge of your life you can *decide* now:
- To respect and love your struggling self, in spite of mistakes, imperfections, lost opportunities.
- To relinquish all the foolish "shoulds" and "oughts" that have nothing to do with life, love, honor, health, or happiness.
- To accept others, including your parents, for the struggling human beings they are.
- To experience I-Thou relationships, free of manipulation.
- To seek self-approval rather than the approval of others.
- To give up the search for glory, vainly trying to satisfy the inner Voice driving you on.
- To be aware of your feelings, but not be overwhelmed by them.
- To assume complete responsibility for your feelings.
- To come on straight, stating your real needs quietly and clearly.
- To give and accept love, and end your fearful isolation.
- To give up claims on perfection, and give yourself permission to experiment and grow.

- To refuse to be vanquished by sorrow.
- To expand your life and stop living within narrow boundaries.
- To live in the only place where time intersects eternity, the here and now.
- To give permission to others:

  to march to their own drummer, be themselves.

  to be less than perfect.

  to disagree with you.

  to own and take full responsibility for their feelings.

- To give yourself permission:

  to listen to your inner conversation.

  to change your inner conversation.

  to assert your God-given rights as an individual.

  to tune down and ignore Not OK Critical Parent messages.

  to make new discoveries about yourself, others, life itself.

  to make mistakes.

  to discontinue repetitive, compulsive behavior.

  to *live*.

I think more of us would take complete charge of our lives if it weren't presented as such a grim task that had best be approached with firm resolve and clenched teeth. One student of mine said he was "sort of happy" and hated to risk it by changing. He was an executive with a large power and light company, and he thought that achieving autonomy implied he would need to change his life style.

The truth of the matter is that autonomous people, those who have found freedom of response, find greater joy, happiness, and self-fulfillment than those who either drift through life or are driven by internal forces over which they have exercised little control. They satisfy their needs more efficiently, they are more comfortable with themselves and others. Such people are more aware of what they want and are able to use their resources to achieve it. They live wholeheartedly, with inner conflicts and divisions kept to a minimum.

The autonomous person has a real self he keeps in touch with, an alive center that he is very much aware of. He is ever mindful that the loss of this real self is, as Kierkegaard said, "a sickness unto death."

The Autonomous Person Protects His Inner Child

The person in charge of his life does not allow his Child to be misused by other people, including his spouse, friends, relatives, or his own children. He knows that people cannot hurt his Child's feelings if he does not *choose* to let them do so. He does not give others remote control of his feelings. When a relative tells him for the fifth or five hundredth time that he has "hurt" that person somehow, the autonomous person decides whether the relative is playing Victim and whether the accusation should be ignored. The autonomous person takes charge of his feelings. His Adult refuses to let others hurt his Child. Nor does the autonomous person take responsibility for the feelings of others. He knows that he *owns* his feelings, and others *own* theirs. If they choose to feel depressed, angry, hopeless, or resentful and invite him to join them, he firmly declines.

The autonomous person also protects his Child from its great expectations. He knows that if victory, applause, adulation, are allowed to send the Child skyrocketing, there will be an inevitable letdown. The autonomous person, to paraphrase Kipling, examines both triumph and disaster, and knows these two are usually impostors.

Three Manifestations of Taking Charge of Your Life

Eric Berne says that "the attainment of autonomy is manifested by the release or recovery of three capacities: awareness, spontaneity and intimacy."* Let's look at each of these manifestations more closely and see what they mean to us.

Awareness

The aware person lives in the here and now. He is accurate in his perceptions; he sees what he is looking at, rather than what he wishes, suspects, hopes, or fears to see. He is able to fill his senses with the object of his attention. He is not on hurry-up time (see Chapter 10). When he is with people, he is *with* them; that is, he *sees* and *hears* them, he absorbs them. He can, for example, actually look at and dwell on a friend's face and be conscious of his friend. He can feel the suffering of another, hear the song of a bird, smell the flowers, delight in a meal.

Aware people keep alert for blind spots within themselves. They test their own perceptions. They keep in touch with reality. The aware person is not only the actor in the play, he is also outside the play and able to observe it. The unaware person is not in attendance at his own life. He cannot be *with* another human being because he is listening to the voice in his head telling him how he's doing or driving him on. His attempts to satisfy this voice, which incessantly calls, "More," "Faster," Better," keep him living in the future. The demands on him are too great for him to consider focusing on the present moment. Like the shopkeeper who hangs the sign on his door: "Here today, out to lunch," the unaware person is there, but not in attendance.

In *The Screwtape Letters,* Screwtape, a devil and an expert in steering humans to perdition, advises his nephew Wormwood, also a devil, on one way to subvert human beings. He doesn't want them aware and living in the present, and tells Wormwood: "It is far better to make them live in the Future. Biological necessity makes all their passions point in that direction already, so that thought

*E. Berne, *Games People Play,* p. 178.

about the Future inflames hope and fear. Also, it is unknown to them, so that in making them think about it we make them think of unrealities."*

Spontaneity

The spontaneous person can change his plans to correspond to the situation he finds himself in. His reactions are fresh and flexible. With the Adult in charge and permitting the other ego states to function and contribute, the spontaneous person can come up with a solution that fits his problem precisely. Awareness permits the autonomous person to absorb his environment, and spontaneity permits him to respond effectively to it. You might find it helpful to think of spontaneity as the quality possessed by a quarterback who, while calling signals at the line of scrimmage, becomes aware of a change in the defense and calls a new play on the spot.

Spontaneity, for the Child within us, means that we have the freedom to choose our feelings. We are not under a compulsion to feel about something the way we were taught we must feel. We can let go, enjoy, have fun, be creative.

Intimacy

James and Jongeward say that "intimacy is expressing the Natural Child feelings of warmth, tenderness, and closeness to others."* Friends, husbands and wives, parents experience intimacy when they are nonjudgmental and acceptant of real feelings. They are then able to enter into warm, disclosing relationships, free of deception, sincere and authentic. When people experience intimacy, they no longer feel they are living in a hostile world, alienated and alone.

When we are intimate we stop playing our role, we drop our

*C. S. Lewis, *The Screwtape Letters* (New York: Macmillan, 1961), p. 68.
*M. James and D. Jongeward, *Born to Win,* p. 255.

mask, we show who we are; we are willing and able to disclose ourselves to someone and let them see the Child hidden inside us with its dreams, hopes, and fears. Invariably, someone asks in a workshop, "But how can I do this at the office?" The answer is: Don't do it at the office. At our present level of organizational behavior, it is definitely an after-office-hours activity. The problem is not that, as human beings, we aren't intimate at the office; the problem is that we are seldom, if ever, intimate with our friends, in our social activities, or even with our loved ones.

Intimacy occurs when two people, alone in a strange universe, reach out and touch each other by saying that which is real to them, that which matters to them as human beings. They say to each other, in effect, "This is me. Take my hand. I am your ally." And then, for just a moment, the darkness beyond the circle of the fire does not matter. We glimpse eternity.

It is odd to what lengths all of us go to avoid closeness with others. It is almost as if we are fearful of touching that from which life itself is made. We engage in frantic social activity because we wish to be near each other, and then carefully structure it so that no matter how long we are together, we learn nothing real about one another. We conduct endless masquerade balls where we hide behind our bright but cool and meaningless conversation.

The Autonomous Person

The autonomous person, in short, has his entire personality, with all its resources, at his disposal. He has access to himself. He is not compartmentalized. He is a free person, free to choose from a wide range of options, not self-condemned to a lifelong search for ever-greater love, security, or glory. He is sensitive to his surroundings and responds to them. He experiences real and authentic relationships.

The man or woman in touch with his ego states who decides to take charge of his personality leads a different life from those who do not.

> "Look, as I blow this feather from my face,
> And as the air blows it to me again,
> Obeying with my wind when I do blow,
> And yielding to another when it blows,
> Commanded always by the greater gust;
> Such is the lightness of you common men."*

The person in charge of his life is no longer "Commanded . . . by the greater gust." He is free, and his reaction when he decides to free himself is joyous: "Look, it's me. I'm back." He remembers that he has forgotten, forgotten that the humane treatment of the self, and all those others out there, is what life is all about. He discovers an ability to enjoy himself, others, and that which he is doing. He is no longer bound by self-imposed limitations on happiness, caught in the self-torture game, seeking approval, listening to harsh tapes, and so he gets closer to life itself —he gets more life from his life.

The Mirror and Your Inner Child

Go to the mirror and look at yourself for a minute. I mean really look at yourself. Remember how once in a great while you have that stunning realization, while looking at yourself, that: "Good Lord, that is really me!" Well, it is, you know, and part of you is that Child inside. For once, see and feel that Child. I don't care if you're eight or eighty, wrinkled or unshaven, middle-aged or a teen-ager, President or pauper; you, I, all of us, have a Child hidden within. And oh, how some of us have mistreated that little person crouched down inside us, wanting so much to be treasured just for ourselves, wanting to be understood, wanting to contribute, wanting to love and be loved. You know that Child's needs. Be kind to him; he represents the very best in you. Love him. Once you feel

*Shakespeare, *Henry VI*, Part 3, Act III, Scene 1.

that inner Child and are kind to him, you become fully functioning, you flourish, you find a new freedom.

Treat that Child in you right, and soon you will find that you're treating others OK too. Your human relations will improve without your being aware of it. Forgive yourself, stop tyrannizing yourself, stop suffering from silly guilt, and you'll stop tyrannizing others. Get in touch with your fears and you'll know about the fears others have. A genuine inner feeling of I'm OK leads to love for others, and this reflects love back to you and then there is no stopping you.

We Are OK and Our Life Has Meaning

You and I *really* are OK, you know. Oh, there is a gap between what man is and what he could be. This has been given many names and includes the belief of many that in some mysterious and not totally explained way, eons ago man was banished to a lesser state than he had held previously. As I write this, my gaze falls on one of the family cats, Tweedle-Dee (an exact copy of her sister, Tweedle-Dum), asleep on some manuscript notes in a shoe box labeled "Finished." She doesn't need to improve; she is always the perfect cat in that her behavior always coincides with her potential. It is we human beings who show the discrepancy between what we are and what we could be. You are OK and so am I, but our behavior does not always reflect this. This difference between man and other animals is what makes ritual forgiveness—Day of Atonement, Absolution—and self-forgiveness so crucially important.

I'm OK—You're OK recognizes the worth of people at the same time it recognizes our faulty behavior. Students never fail to reply to that: "You can't forgive all faulty behavior. What about Hitler?" My answer is: Don't start with Hitler. He and other hardened criminals are too difficult for us. Make them your exceptions if you wish. Start with your annoying neighbor down the street, and work up from there.

The future of civilization depends on all of us making the I'm

OK—You're OK decision, recognizing that man is of supreme importance and that we do not live in isolation from one another. Failing this decision, we create our own personal misery and, in addition, make the struggle to improve mankind meaningless. The OK—OK position gives meaning to all we do—our education, our system of justice, our struggle for freedom (the emphasis on brotherly love), our cultural activities, our very lives—and makes the effort to improve our mental health, our behavior, important.

Without this meaning, we lose that which is most precious to man; we become mere animals. As Viktor Frankl, the Austrian psychiatrist who was a prisoner in Nazi concentration camps, said:

If we present a man with a concept of man which is not true, we may well corrupt him. When we present man as an automation of reflexes, as a mind-machine, as a bundle of instincts, as a pawn of drives and reactions, as a mere product of instinct, heredity, and environment, we feed the nihilism to which modern man is, in any case, prone.

I became acquainted with the last stage of that corruption in my second concentration camp, Auschwitz. The gas chambers of Auschwitz were the ultimate consequence of the theory that man is nothing but the product of heredity and environment—or, as the Nazi liked to say, of "Blood and Soil." I am absolutely convinced that the gas chambers of Auschwitz, Treblinka, and Maidanek were ultimately prepared not in some Ministry or other in Berlin, but rather at the desks and in the lecture halls of nihilistic scientists and philosophers.*

Where Do We Go from Here?

Well, that's it. That's what I wanted to share with you. We've come a long way together in this book, and I hope by this time you are already doing those things we talked about in different chapters. I'd like to repeat: TA has given me, my family, and many, many others a new way of life; and it doesn't happen by making impossible resolutions, setting unrealistic goals or wrestling for the

*V. Frankl, *The Doctor and the Soul: From Psychotherapy to Logotherapy*, trans. Richard and Clara Winston, 2d ed. (New York: Alfred A. Knopf, 1955, 1965), pages xviii and xix in The Introduction.

thousandth time with our fears, worries, guilt, anger, greed, lack of assertiveness, extreme aggression, or whatever. No, TA helps you understand yourself once you start listening to those tapes, getting in touch with your Child, giving more power to your Adult, changing your stroking patterns, self-contracting, and doing the other things I have covered in this book. And then you look around you one day, and lo and behold, you find you are getting more from your life, you're happier, you handle everything more effectively.

It's up to you, of course, but I'd like you to consider rereading those parts that were especially important to you. I'd also like you to discuss parts of the book with a friend or someone you love, or in a group. You might wish to consider joining a TA group after checking the credentials of the therapist who leads it. They can be interesting and enjoyable. All these activities are called reinforcement, but all it means is that you, in your Adult, have decided to invest a little time in making yourself more effective, giving yourself freedom, independence, and joy.

As you apply TA in your life, it will continue to improve. With this improvement will come a soaring of spirit and a freedom you have never known before, and among other benefits to you, you will bestow upon yourself a mantle of joy and self-determination such as Yeats desired for his daughter when he wrote:

> "Considering that, all hatred driven hence,
> The soul recovers radical innocence
> And learns at last that it is self-delighting,
> Self-appeasing, self-affrighting,
> And that its own sweet will is Heaven's will;
> She can, though every face should scowl
> And every windy quarter howl
> Or every bellows burst, be happy still.*

*W. B. Yeats, "A Prayer For My Daughter," *Collected Poems,* 2d ed. (New York: Macmillan, 1956).

Index